MAKING
OLD TESTAMENT
TOYS

MARGARET HUTCHINGS

with illustrations by
the author

MILLS & BOON LIMITED
LONDON

TAPLINGER
PUBLISHING COMPANY
NEW YORK

Other books by the same author

The "What Shall I Do?" series, "Modern Soft Toy Making", etc.

First published in Great Britain in 1972 by Mills & Boon Limited, 17–19 Foley Street, London W1A 1DR

First published in the United States in 1972 by the Taplinger Publishing Co Inc, New York

British ISBN 0 263.05006.8

American ISBN 0-8008-5079-3

Library of Congress Catalog Number 78–185484

Made and printed in Great Britain by Morrison and Gibb Ltd, London and Edinburgh

Contents

This little book could only
be dedicated to
EMMA LUCY
because she's the best thing
that ever happened—at least
since her father and uncles!

Foreword

I wonder if you are like me and things you either don't understand or cannot change appear in your mind as very definite shapes, colours and sometimes smells! My "year" is a long narrow line which curves gently downwards from January to June, runs straight through July and August, then careers madly upwards to Christmas Day when it stops. I see nothing between Christmas and January—just a blank. On the other hand I have a friend whose "year" spins round and round in an everlasting circle.

When I was very small the Bible was a heavy dark "lump" which smelt musty—I hated and avoided it. Over the course of my life and due mainly I believe to a wonderful grandmother who knew her Bible inside out and talked in a "real" and open way of its characters, this book has become a "bright-coloured best seller" in my mind, out of which tumble fascinating, colourful stories and characters in every shape and size. It's all there for the reading—love, adventure, history, geography, architecture, archaeology, zoology, natural history, comedy, tragedy, adventure, intrigue, war and crime. I have decided that if I were ever marooned on Roy Plomley's desert island I would take with me my "Con-cordance" so that using it with the Bible I would find already there, I should be kept happily occupied for the rest of my life unravelling and sorting it all out! If I could have a box of sewing materials, pencils and paints as well, I could carry on

making more of the hundreds of characters I should have liked to include in this little book, but which its size does not permit.

If *your* Bible is still a "heavy dark lump", I hope these ideas will help to change it for you. They are intended for everyone—for teachers and pupils, mothers and daughters, grannies and grandchildren, godparents and godchildren. None of the toys are exhibition pieces but all of them are simple so that even the youngest member of the family can join in.

M.H.

GENERAL INSTRUCTIONS

1. It is worth while tracing the patterns on to thin cardboard and cutting out a template to draw round. In this way your work will be more accurate and you can label and keep the pieces for future use.

2. Unless otherwise stated Copydex or Elmer's Glue-all is ideal for all the sticking. Use it sparingly and on tiny parts such as eyes dab on with a cocktail stick. Paper clips are often useful to hold parts together while adhesive dries.

3. Follow the picture of the toy you are constructing all the time you are working, especially when making faces and other details.

4. A series of strips of paper will be useful for "book marks". You can then turn quickly back to any pictures or instructions referred to in various parts of the book without constantly searching for a certain page.

5. Flesh pink or fawn felt will do equally well for skin. Most of the people in these stories were probably a most attractive sun-bronzed coffee colour. Most of their clothes were natural linen and wool colours, but they also produced scarlet dye from a special insect (rather like our cochineal), "rose madder" from the madder plant, yellow from almonds; and the Canaanites or Phoenicians made expensive purple cloth from shellfish —so if I were you I'd dress the characters in just whatever I happened to have handy and let my imagination run riot, which is more fun than always trying to be correct.

6. Always read right through the instructions for whatever you have decided to make before starting to work, making sure you have all you need and that you understand them—then don't be afraid to branch out and experiment.

7. Start to save lolly sticks, (popsicle sticks), spools and reels, matchboxes, scraps of gold or silver cardboard, tubes from toilet rolls, cream and yoghurt cartons, tissue paper, scraps of knitting wool and old tights—you will need them as you work through the book.

8. All biblical references are taken from the Revised Version.

NOTE TO AMERICAN READERS

The following terms or references may be unfamiliar to American readers of this book. Accordingly short descriptions are supplied below:

bass or garden bass—a woody fiber

cocktail stick—or a tooth pick

colourless gum—gum tragacanth

furnishing fabric—upholstery or drapery fabric

lurex—fabric with metallic threads

oddment—remnant

postcard—as an index or file card

scrip—a small bag or wallet carried by a wayfarer

stiletto—a small pointed instrument for making eyelet holes

template—a pattern to serve as a gauge or guide

THE CREATION

"In the beginning God created the heaven and the earth." (Genesis 1.1)

When you read the story of the creation do you find it difficult to remember in what order everything was made? I do. I thought it would be helpful to make a flannelgraph, thus turning it into a sort of puzzle. When you have finished you will have a picture like the one on pages 8 and 9. You can take it to pieces and see how quickly you can build it up again.

YOU WILL NEED

A piece of strong cardboard roughly the size of this book when opened out flat, i.e. about 7×10 inches (18×26 cm).
A large piece of thick dark navy material to cover it. Oddments of felt in *light blue* for day: *darker blue* for sea: various shades of *green* for grass, bushes, tree and fig leaves: *fawn* for earth: *brown* for tree trunk and hair: *pale pink* for Adam and Eve: *grey* for goat and fish: *black* for birds: *orange* for sun: *red* for apples: *yellow* for sand and moon: *white* for flowers: *tawny gold* for lion.
A pipe cleaner for the serpent.
Silver paper or Lurex material for stars.

HOW TO MAKE IT

Follow the picture all the time; this is drawn actual size so that you can trace the pieces from it. You will easily be able to guess the shape of the pieces overlapped.

1. Cut out the goat, lion, fig leaves, Adam and Eve, their hair, fish, tree, tree trunk, apples, birds, sun, moon, stars, flowers, grass and bushes.

2. Cover the board with the navy material, turning it over to the back and securing with criss-cross stitches in strong thread (Fig. 1).

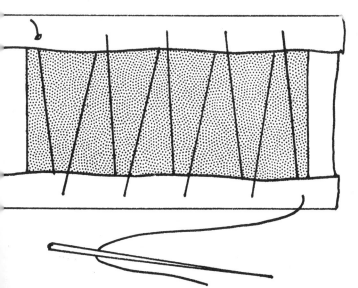

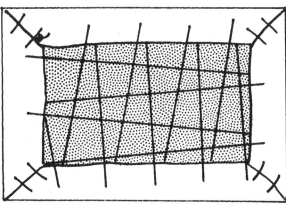

Fig. 1 Covering a board with material.

"And the earth was without form . . . and darkness was upon the face of the deep." (Genesis 1.2)

3. Cut a piece of sky blue felt half the size of the board and lay it on the left hand side.

". . . And God said 'Let there be light' . . . and called the light Day and the darkness he called Night." (Genesis 1.3 and 5)

4. This blue piece also serves for the firmament or sky so do not add another piece yet.

". . . . let there be a firmament in the midst of the waters and let it divide the waters from the waters . . . and he called the firmament Heaven." (Genesis 1.6)

5. Cut a piece of fawn felt for earth and lay it on board.

6. Cut a piece of yellow felt for sand and tuck it along behind the top of the earth.

7. Cut a piece of bright blue felt for sea and tuck it along behind the sand.

". . . let the waters under the heavens be gathered together into one place and let the dry land appear . . ." (Genesis 1.9)

8. Add the grass, bushes, tree, apples and flowers.

". . . let the earth bring forth grass, the herb yielding seed and fruit tree yielding fruit . . ." (Genesis 1.11)

9. Add the sun, moon and stars.

". . . the greater light to rule the day and the lesser light to rule the night; He made the stars also . . ." (Genesis 1.16)

10. Add the fish and birds.

" . . . let the waters bring forth abundantly the moving creature that hath life and fowl that may fly above the earth . . ." (Genesis 1.20)

11. Add the goat, lion and serpent.

"Let the earth bring forth the living creature after his kind, cattle and creeping thing and beast of the earth . . ." (Genesis 1.24)

12. Add Adam, his hair and fig-leaf skirt.

"—Let us make man in our image after our likeness . . . but it is not good that man shall be alone. I will make him a help meet for him . . ." (Genesis 1.26 and 2.18)

13. Add Eve, her hair and skirt.

" . . . a deep sleep fell upon Adam and while he slept God took one of his ribs . . . which he made into a woman." (Genesis 2.21 and 22)

———

A quick guide to help you when using your flannelgraph.
Add: Darkness; Day/night; (firmament); earth/sea; plants/fruit trees/flowers; sun/moon/stars; fish/birds; animals; man; woman— in that order. Look at the cover picture for colours.

A Woolly Caterpillar

"... caterpillars came without number."   (Psalm 105.34)

We shall never know what these caterpillars looked like so I thought we'd make a "pretend" one—big, fat and wicked!

YOU WILL NEED

Tissue paper and oddments of bright coloured wool for the body.
Some scraps of fur.
Two coloured beads and two white buttons for eyes.
A pipe cleaner and two smaller coloured beads for "feelers".
Black wool for "mouth".

HOW TO MAKE HIM

1. *Body and Head:* Make seven or more woollen balls about the size of a golf ball as shown on page 46 for the owl (Fig. 31). Use two gay colours.

2. *Feelers:* Thread the two small beads on to the pipe cleaner (Fig. 2A). Bend the cleaner back and twist it round itself at each end

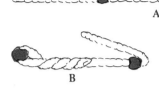

Fig. 2   Making the Caterpillar's feelers.

(2B) thus securing the beads. Bend ends upwards and sew firmly to one of the balls (2C). This is top of head.

3. Sew the buttons and beads in place for eyes and embroider "mouth".

4. Using strong thread and a long needle take a few stitches on back of head, then thread on the rest of the balls, taking alternate colours. Fasten off thread securely by stitching at end of last ball and stick or glue a scrap of fur to each section.

" ... that which the palmer worm hath left hath the locust eaten; and that which the locust hath left hath the cankerworm eaten; and that which the cankerworm hath left hath the caterpillar eaten."

(Joel 1.4)

The Plague of Frogs

" . . . the river shall bring forth frogs abundantly which shall go up and come into thine house and into thy bedchamber and upon thy bed . . . and into thine ovens and into thy kneading troughs . . .'

(Exodus 8.3)

The story of the ten plagues that God sent upon the Egyptians to try to secure the deliverance of the Israelites is well known, and the second of these was of course the plague of frogs. This is a happy friendly frog who can be pushed and pulled into any position.

YOU WILL NEED

Two pieces of cotton material each at least $6 \times 4\frac{1}{2}$ inches (11×16 cm) (preferably yellow for "tummy" and green for back). Two round beads for eyes. A handful of rice for filling.

HOW TO MAKE HIM

1. Cut out a cardboard pattern (pattern page 85).

2. Place this on the wrong side of one of the pieces of material and pencil clearly all round it.

3. Place this piece of material on top of the other, right sides inside. Pin here and there to hold in place.

4. Machine all round on the pencil line except between A and B. Cut out leaving small turning.

5. Clip a little way into corners such as C, D, E, etc. Turn right side out, pushing out arms and legs with the knob end of a knitting needle.

6. Using a teaspoon, fill *loosely* with rice leaving sufficient empty space to make the frog very pliable.

7. Sew up opening A–B.

8. Sew on eyes.

9. Shake rice into tips of arms and legs and bend your frog to "sit" how you wish.

———

" . . . the frogs died out of the houses, out of the villages and out of the fields. And they gathered them together upon heaps: and the land stank." (Exodus 8.13, 14)

Ugh!

The Locust

" . . . when it was morning the east
wind brought the locusts."
(Exodus 10.13)

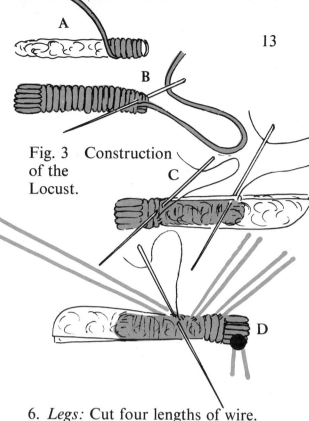

Fig. 3 Construction
of the
Locust.

Another of the plagues sent to
harrow the Egyptians were the
dreaded swarms of locusts which
ate up every growing thing within
sight. These nasty creatures look
rather like a grasshopper.

YOU WILL NEED

A scrap of tissue
    paper   for the
A few yards of   body.
    green wool
A short piece of *thin* green plastic-
covered gardener's wire for legs.
Two small round beads for eyes.
Tiny scrap of white or green dress
net for wings.

HOW TO MAKE HIM

1. Cut out the wings (pattern
page 93) (2 pieces).

2. *Body:* Crumple the tissue paper
tightly into a little "tube" about
$2 \times \frac{1}{2}$ inch (5×1.5 cm) Fig. (3A).

3. Bind this all over with green
wool (A) finishing off both "ends"
by stitching over and over and
making the head end a little fatter
by extra binding (B).

4. *Wings:* Sew a wing to each side
of body. Overlap and catch at tail
end of body (C).

5. *Eyes:* Sew on bead eyes (D).

6. *Legs:* Cut four lengths of wire.
1 inch for feelers, 3 inches for
forelegs, $6\frac{1}{2}$ inches for hindlegs,
$3\frac{1}{2}$ inches for centre pair of legs:
($2 \cdot 5$ cm, $7 \cdot 5$ cm, $16 \cdot 5$ cm and 9 cm).

7. Fold each piece in half. Sew
"feelers" to top of head. Sew the
three "pairs" of legs in place to
underside of body (D). Then bend
each pair to position shown on
picture, adjusting your locust to
stand firmly.

Locusts were used widely for food
in Old-Testament times—the
Assyrians served them on skewers
rather like our present-day Kebabs.

" . . . Ye may eat the locust after
his kind, and the bald locust after
his kind, and the beetle and the
grasshopper . . ."   (Leviticus 11.22)

"Upon thy belly shalt thou go and dust shalt thou eat all the days of thy life." (Genesis 3.14)

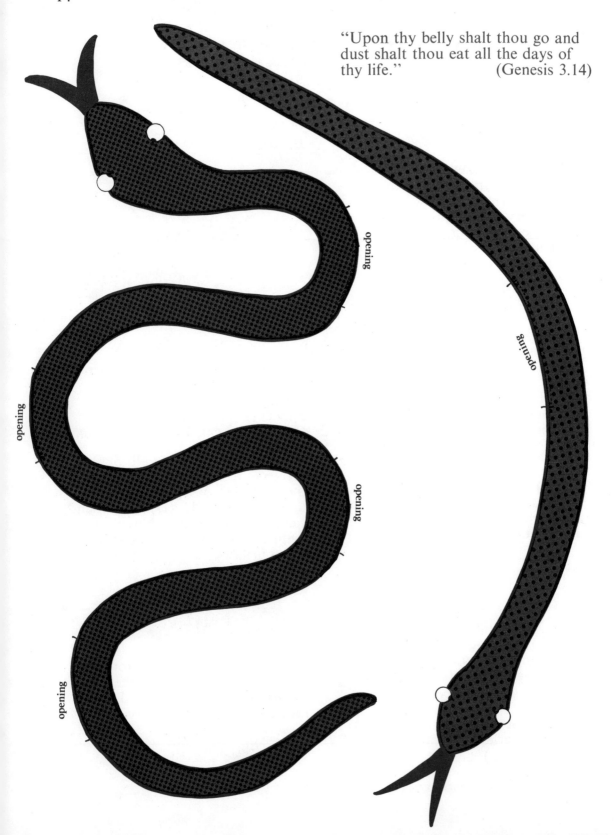

opening

opening

opening

opening

opening

opening

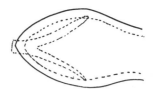

Two Serpents

"Now the serpent was more subtil than any other beast of the field . . ."
(Genesis 3.1)

Throughout the Bible the serpent (or snake as we know it) is constantly connected with craftiness and subtlety. The poor thing is cursed over and over again and even today not many of us are fond of these uncanny, slithering beasts. The serpents on the opposite page feel creepy when you hold them because they are filled with rice.

FOR THE STRAIGHT ONE
YOU WILL NEED

Two strips of bright coloured cotton material at least 20 × 2 inches (51 × 5 cm).
Two round beads for eyes.
A scrap of felt for tongue.
Rice for filling.

HOW TO MAKE HIM

1. Cut out body and tongue in card (patterns page 95).

2. Make up exactly as given for frog on page 12 but place the tongue forked side inside at point of head (Fig. 4) before machining so that when turned right side out it will protrude from mouth and be securely fixed.

"They have sharpened their tongues like a serpent: adders' poison is under their lips."   (Psalm 140.3)

Fig. 4   Serpent's tongue placed inside head when stitching.

FOR THE CROOKED SERPENT
YOU WILL NEED

The same materials as for the straight one but larger pieces of material—at least 24 × 8 inches (61 × 21 cm).

HOW TO MAKE HIM

Using head, tail and tongue patterns on page 95 draw shape of body between head and tail by placing a saucer first one side then the other of an imaginary straight line and drawing round it (Fig. 5). Do not draw the serpent too narrow or you will find him very difficult to fill. Make him exactly as the straight serpent but leave an opening on every curve: clip into curves before turning.

Fig. 5   Shaping body of Crooked Serpent.

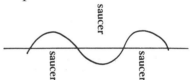

There are several references to "the crooked serpent" but they do not signify a wicked, wiggly snake like the one we have made but rather a great sea monster.

" . . . the Lord . . . shall punish . . . the piercing serpent . . . even Leviathan that crooked serpent."
(Isaiah 27.1)

The crooked serpent and Leviathan are also other names for the devil. We'll make Leviathan next.

Leviathan

" . . . Out of his mouth go burning lamps, and sparks of fire leap out . . . He esteemeth iron as straw and brass as rotten wood . . . He maketh the deep to boil like a pot: he maketh the sea like a pot of ointment . . ."   (Job 41.19, 27, 31)

A fearsome monster indeed and this whole chapter is a thrilling description of everyone's idea of a gigantic, majestic and mighty sea creature. It is of course difficult to say just what Leviathan really was —some say a whale, some a crocodile—or he may have been something quite unknown to us rather like the Loch Ness Monster! Let's use this chapter of Job to make ourselves a nonesuch imaginary creature of the sea.

YOU WILL NEED

8 empty matchboxes and the tray part of two others.
Bright green or other colour felt to cover them.
White postcard for teeth.
Two large, thin buttons for eyes (about ¾ inch (2 cm) diameter).
Tiny scraps of black felt for pupils, red for nostrils and "flame".

A piece of white net for "breath" 10 × 8 inches (26 × 20cm).

A few small beads and a piece of fuse wire for "smoke".
A pipe cleaner to stiffen "flame".

HOW TO MAKE HIM

1. Cut out scales, pupils, teeth, nostrils and flame (10 pieces without scales) (patterns page 86).

2. *Body:* Prepare and cover the eight matchboxes following Fig. 6. (A) Stuff each box with tissue paper. (B) Stretch a strip of felt round the box and oversew along one edge. (C) Oversew a rectangle to each end.

3. Fix them together in the positions shown in the picture by first sticking or glueing and then stitching by working a sort of ladder stitch— one stitch on one box, then one on the other (D).

" . . . That crooked serpent."
(Isaiah 27.1)

4. *Head:* Completely cover the two empty trays both inside and out. (E) Stick a piece of felt round the box widthwise, covering bottom

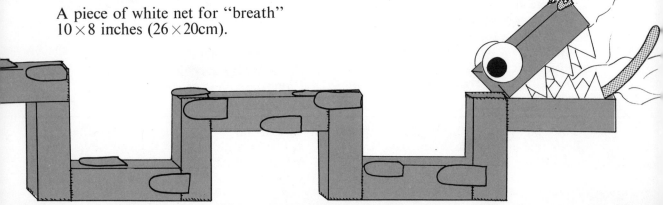

and sides inside out. (F) Stick on two narrower pieces to cover ends inside and out.

5. Oversew these two trays together on the inside for head and open mouth (G).

Fig. 6 Preparing matchboxes.

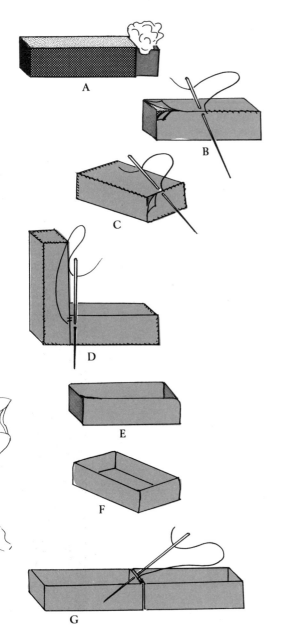

"Who can open the doors of his face? . . ." (Job 41.14)

6. Stick and stitch this piece in place to top, front of first box of body. (Look at picture.)

7. *Eyes:* Stick pupils to eyes and one eye to each side of head.

" . . . his eyes are like the eyelids of the morning . . ." (Job 41.18)

8. *Smoke:* (Fig. 7A) Thread 12–18 small beads on to a piece of fuse wire. (B) Twist one end back round and round. (C) Thread both ends through centre of nostril. (D) Secure at back with a tiny piece of adhesive tape. (E) Cut off surplus wire. Make another in the same way and stick nostrils to top front corners of upper jaw.

"Out of his nostrils goeth smoke as out of a seething pot or cauldron." (Job 41.20)

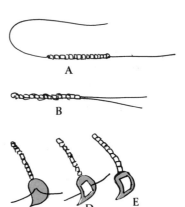

Fig. 7 Making Leviathan's smoke.

9. Stick the teeth along the inside of each side of both jaws, thus propping the mouth open.

" . . . his teeth are terrible round about . . ." (Job 41.14)

10. *Flame:* Stick the two "flame" pieces together with a piece of pipe cleaner between them to stiffen. Curl one end gently upwards and stick in place to inside of lower "jaw".

" . . . and a flame goeth out of his mouth." (Job 41.21)

11. *Breath:* Fold the net loosely in half widthwise and stick into mouth on top of flame.

" . . . his breath kindleth coals . . ." (Job 41.21)

12. Stick the scales singly and in groups here and there all over body.

" . . . his scales are his pride . . ." (Job 41.15)

———

You can of course add more matchboxes and make Leviathan longer.

"Upon earth there is not his like, who is made without fear . . ." (Job 41.33)

Again you can make him several heads—the Psalmist mentions them in the plural " . . . thou breakest the heads of Leviathan in pieces . . ." (Psalm 74.14) and the Canaanites in their myths depicted him as having seven!

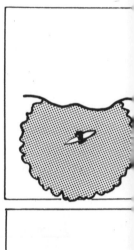

The Israelites crossing THE RED SEA

Fig. 9   (on left)
Back of the model.

"The children of Israel went into the midst of the sea upon the dry ground: and the waters were a wall unto them on their right hand and on their left."   (Exodus 14.22)

The story of the crossing of the Red Sea always conjures up in my mind vivid pictures of a path through a swirling, wicked-looking sea of bright red water. I thought it would be fun to make a working model like this—although of course we all know that the water in the Red Sea is really just like any other water. This model costs nothing to make.

Fig. 8   The revolving circle.

YOU WILL NEED

2 pieces of strong cardboard about the size of this book—(top and bottom of a stocking box?)
A pile of old magazines with coloured pictures.
One paper fastener.

HOW TO MAKE IT

1. Go through the magazines and cut out all the streaky or plain red paper you can find—the more different shades of red the better. You can use all sorts of shapes cut from pictures of curtains, carpets, sunsets, large flowers, clothes, etc.

2. Cut out a large pile of small heads and shoulders of people, singly or in groups. If possible find one or two in Arab dress and a horse or camel—travel brochures are useful. If you can find one cut out a seagull too.

3. From a piece of card cut a circle $5\frac{1}{2}$ inches (14 cm) across (or use a saucer as a pattern).

4. Stick or glue the cut-out people all over the outside $1\frac{1}{2}$ inches (4 cm), massed together one on top of the other, heads outwards, waists inwards (Fig. 8).

5. Cut round the tops of their heads so that the edge of the card does not show.

6. Look at the picture and on the other piece of card stick the red cut-out pieces to look like a rough sea, starting about 4 inches (10 cm) from the top and working down-wards. Make the top edge uneven for waves.

7. With a sharp knife cut a slit following the outline of the top edge of waves, about $5\frac{1}{2}$ inches (14 cm) across at centre (Fig. 9). Try your circular piece by slipping it through the slit and revolving it. Make sure that about $1\frac{1}{4}$ (4 cm) of the "children of Israel" show on the front as the circle revolves.

8. Put circle on one side. Look at picture and leaving a "gap" for the dry path across the sea, stick on more red water—a straight edge along base and rolling waves along top.

9. Stick more people, camels, etc. on each side of where the circle will revolve so as to almost fill the dry path.

10. Fix the circle in place loosely with a paper fastener.

11. Cut out and stick a few arms, legs, hands and perhaps a fish or two among the waves, a seagull in the sky and a tiny red cloud. If you like you can paint the sky blue and what shows of the dry path, yellow for sand.

When you turn the circle you will have the people crossing the dry path in an endless stream—the cloud that they followed hovering over them, whilst the Egyptians drown in the sea below! It does not matter that your Israelites are in modern dress—because massed together they just look like "people".

"A pillar of cloud to lead them by the way; and by night a pillar of fire to give them light . . .'
(Exodus 13.21)

A CAMEL from matchboxes

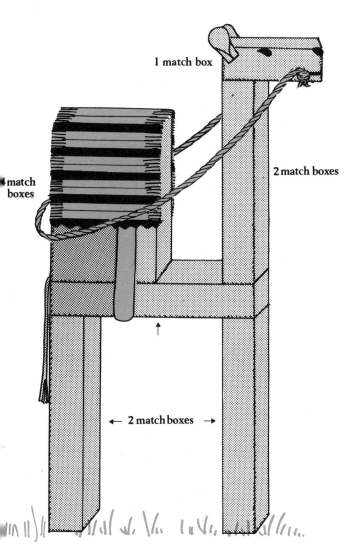

1 match box

2 match boxes

4 match boxes

← 2 match boxes →

" . . . I will draw water for thy camels also, until they have done drinking." (Genesis 24.19)

Camels were of course invaluable to traders because of their ability to go without food and water for days on end and thus travel long distances across the desert. Their hair too was useful for making extra coarse cloth for bags, tents and cloaks. What a pity these creatures are so stupid and bad tempered.

The camel shown below is the one humped variety and to make him

YOU WILL NEED

13 empty matchboxes and sufficient camel coloured felt to cover them.
Scraps of black felt for eyes and nostrils.
Black stranded embroidery cotton for mouth.
Cord for reins.
Bright material for saddle cloth and felt for girth.

HOW TO MAKE HIM

1. Cut out ears, eyes, nostrils and tail (patterns page 86) (7 pieces).

2. *Body:* Prepare and cover the matchboxes as on pages 16 and 17 for Leviathan No. 2, Fig. 6 A, B and C, using one for the head, two placed end to end and stuck together

with Sellotape or Scotch tape before covering, for body, legs and neck, and four piled one on top of each other for hump.

3. Stick and stitch them together following picture for positions and consulting page 16, No. 3 and Fig. 6 D for method.

4. *Ears:* Fold base of ears inwards and stick in this position (Fig. 10).

Fig. 10   Folding Camel's ear.

5. Stick ears, tail, eyes and nostrils to camel.

6. *Mouth:* Embroider mouth using stranded cotton and a long, strong needle, working right through box (Fig. 11).

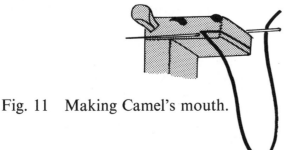

Fig. 11   Making Camel's mouth.

7. *Finishing off:* Stick and/or stitch on reins, saddle cloth and a felt girth.

————

You can if you wish load his hump with merchandise such as little rolls of cloth (Fig. 12) or small net bags slung on each side and filled with a

few dried peas for olives. (These bags are easy to make from the nylon nets in which oranges or nuts are sold.)

Fig. 12   Rolls of cloth for Camel's back.

One of the only times we hear of camels being used for war is when the Midianites attacked Israel, burning and killing. " . . . for both they and their camels were without number and they entered into the land to destroy it."   (Judges 6.5)

Fig. 13   Folding Ass's ear.

Fig. 14   Making saddle bag.

AN ASS from matchboxes

"And Abraham rose up early . . . and saddled his ass . . ." (Genesis 22.3)

Abraham needed his ass to carry wood—this lovable creature, better known to you and me as a donkey, was the most useful and loyal of all animals. He was used for everything, farm work, carrying burdens and riding, as well as being a sort of "wealth" symbol—one's riches being counted by the number of animals owned. Almost every well-off family possessed at least one ass just as today they would have a car. To make this rather dejected "donkey"

YOU WILL NEED

6 empty matchboxes and sufficient grey felt to cover them.

Black felt for eyes and nostrils.
Black stranded embroidery cotton for mouth.
Bright coloured wool for reins and bridle.
Grey fur or fringe for mane.
Scrap of bright material for saddle cloth.
Empty roll from toilet paper and bright felt for saddle bags.

HOW TO MAKE HIM

1. Cut out the ears, eyes, nostrils, saddle-bag strap and tail (patterns page 87) (8 pieces).

Now work from numbers 2–6 exactly as given for camel on pages 21 and 22, but following picture below for number of match-boxes, noting different way to fold ear (Fig. 13) and adding a fur mane.

7. Stick saddle cloth in place.

8. *Reins:* Tie on bridle and one leading rein, using bright coloured wool.

9. *Saddle bags:* Cut two rings $1\frac{1}{4}$ inches (4 cm) wide from an empty toilet roll tube and squash and fold each piece so that it is

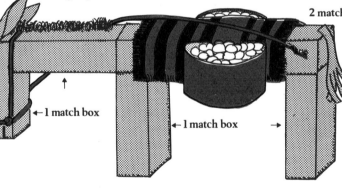

2 match boxes

←1 match box

←1 match box→

D-shaped and has one flat side. (Look at picture.) Stick a piece of bright-coloured felt all round each saddle bag, having the join in centre of flat side. Cut a D-shaped piece of the same felt to fit base and oversew this in place all round lower edge (Fig. 14).

10. Stick the saddle-bag strap just inside the flat back of each bag. Fill with dried peas (for olives) and hang across ass's back.

" . . . he will take . . . your asses and put them to his work."

(1 Samuel 8.16)

A curly sheep and her lamb

"What meaneth this bleating of
sheep in my ears?"

(1 Samuel 15.14)

Sheep turn up again and again in
every part of the Bible. One can
easily imagine their value—warm
fleece for clothing and delicious
meat to roast on the open fires.

YOU WILL NEED

Approximately 26 pipe cleaners for
legs and fleece.
A small piece of very strong, white
cardboard for body.
Black drawing ink.
A scrap of black felt for ears.

HOW TO MAKE HIM

1. Cut out the body and ears
(3 pieces), pattern page 86.

2. Paint nose and eyes on both
sides of card, allow to dry.

3. Stick on ears.

4. *Legs:* Twist two pipe cleaners
together (Fig. 15A). Push them
through one of the leg holes. Bend
downwards flat against body (B),
having an even length at each side.
Bend each piece back up on itself
(C) and twist together, so that
each leg consists of four thicknesses
of pipe cleaner (D). Make the other
pair of legs in the same way.

5. *Fleece:* Make a series of small
holes all over body—approximately
40. They should be so small that it
is difficult to push a pipe cleaner
through and they fit very tightly.

6. Cut the pipe cleaners in half,
making 44 pieces. Starting at the
top of the head, push half a cleaner
through a hole and fold flat upwards
against card (E). Starting at the end,
roll each cleaner downwards
between finger and thumb (F and
G). Press flat against card to form a
curl (H). Roll the other half in the
same way, flat on to other side of
card (I).

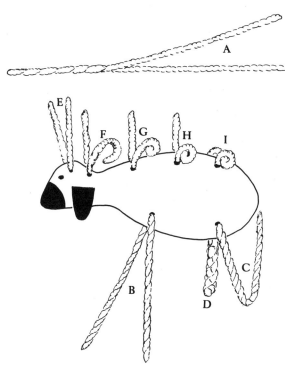

Fig. 15   Construction of Sheep.

HOW TO MAKE THE LAMB

Work exactly as for the sheep but use smaller patterns (page 87) and fewer pipe cleaners. Give him a tail. Bend the legs to give him a skipping appearance.

" . . . the little hills skipped like lambs."   (Psalm 114.4)

David was of course the most famous shepherd of all time. The next page shows how to make him.

"And David rose up early in the morning and left the sheep with a keeper . . . and he came to the trench as the host was going forth to the fight, and shouted for the battle."   (1 Samuel 17.20)

7. Work in this way until your sheep is completely covered with curls. Make sure that the ends of legs and ears are covered, also the edges of card so that the sheep has a soft "woolly" outline. The eyes should be almost buried. If necessary make a few more holes and add more pipe cleaners.

8. Paint the legs black with drawing ink and when dry adjust your sheep to stand firmly.

———

"If a man shall steal an ox or a sheep and kill it or sell it, he shall restore five oxen for an ox and four sheep for a sheep."   (Exodus 22.1)

DAVID AND GOLIATH—
a working model

" . . . David prevailed over the Philistine with a sling and with a stone and smote him and slew him; but there was no sword in the hand of David . . ." (1 Samuel 17.50)

David and Goliath are perfect subjects for a working model which moves backwards and forwards so that they appear to be fighting.

YOU WILL NEED

Firm, strong cardboard for all the pieces.
A scrap of material for David's tunic.
A scrap of leather or felt for his sling and scrip.
4 paper fasteners to join the model.
A few extra paper fasteners to decorate Goliath's armour.

HOW TO MAKE IT

1. Cut out David, Goliath, the sling, scrip, and two cardboard strips 13 × ¾ inches (33 × 2 cm) (patterns, pages 91 and 92) (6 pieces). If this is too difficult in strong card, cut two of each piece in thinner card and stick them firmly together.

2. *David:* Paint David flesh colour all over. Then add brown or black hair and sandals either by painting or sticking on felt sandals and thongings and wool hair.

3. Drape a piece of rough weave material round his body for a tunic and stick in place in front at neck and here and there at back.

4. Tie a piece of string round waist for girdle—sticking at back.

5. Fold scrip in half along broken line and tuck one half behind girdle, then stick the two pieces together. Pull scrip backwards so that it is "flying outwards" and stick to tunic in this position.

6. Twist sling round wrist (look at picture). Stick in place front and back. Stick the other end to back of head, leaving the long piece between loose.

7. *Goliath:* Read the description of Goliath in 1 Samuel 17.5 and colour the cardboard figure as you wish, " . . . and he had a helmet of brass upon his head" etc. Decorate the armour with paper fastener studs. (If you prefer, you can stick material, or coloured card or leather, to the figure for clothes.) Make a spear with a lightweight knitting needle, piece of wood or strong card and fix firmly to back of figure with Evostik or other strong glue, and, for extra strength, small pieces of adhesive tape.

8. *Finishing off:* Using a needlework stiletto if possible, pierce holes in the card strips and on David and Goliath's legs as shown on pattern.

9. Look at picture. Fix figures loosely to the strips with four paper fasteners, putting a small circular cardboard "washer" between each limb and strip to help the model work smoothly.

10. Take each "handle" between a thumb and forefinger. Hold the right hand still and move the left backwards and forwards.

"David put his hand in his bag and took thence a stone and slang it and smote the Philistine that the stone sunk into his forehead; and he fell upon his face to the earth . . ."
(1 Samuel 17.49)

BEHEMOTH (the elephant)

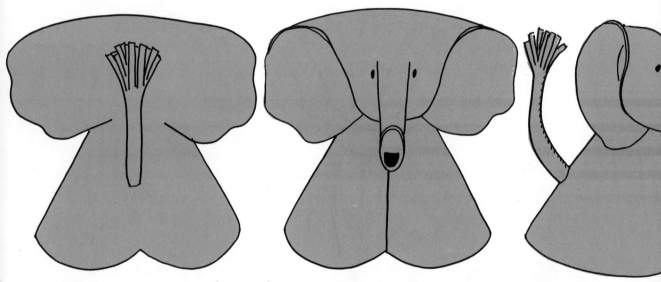

"He eateth grass as an ox . . . his bones are as strong pieces of brass —behold he drinketh up a river and hasteth not: he trusteth that he can draw up Jordan into his mouth . . ."
(Job 40.15 etc.)

Do read these few fascinating verses and decide whether you think this description of "Behemoth" given by God to Job refers to the elephant or, as some think, the hippopotamus— "drawing up Jordan into his mouth" makes *me* sure it's the elephant.

We read of ivory or elephant's tusks being brought by the navy from Tarshish (1 Kings 10.22) and even of ivory beds (Amos 6.4) and an ivory house (1 Kings 22.39) the remains of which were actually found in Samaria in 1935. My elephant is simply made by a series of folds—he does not have tusks.

YOU WILL NEED

Part of an old felt hat.
Two tiny black beads for eyes.

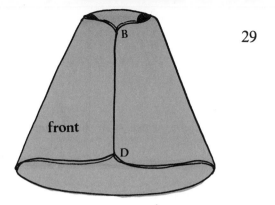

Fig. 16   Front of Elephant's body.

HOW TO MAKE HIM

1. Cut the hat in half. Thoroughly wash the two pieces. Squeeze out all surplus water. Press with a hot iron under a cloth, pulling to flatten and get rid of "shape" and bulge of crown. Finish drying on a flat surface in a warm place.

2. Cut out the body, head and tail (3 pieces). (Patterns page 89.)

3. *Body:* Roll the body round so that the A's and B's meet and on the wrong side oversew A–B. Turn right side out and tuck in the flap C–E–C to fill top hole (Fig. 16). Pinch front seam inwards so that D's join and catch together here (Fig. 17). This "tuck" is at the front.

4. *Head:* Roll the trunk round so that the F's and G's meet and oversew this seam on the right side —this comes underneath trunk. Sew the two beads in place for eyes. Fold this head piece in half so that the broken line H–H comes along top of head and the flap J–G–J rests behind top of trunk—G's matching. Stab stitch J–G–J (Fig. 18).

5. Invisibly stitch head to body— the flap J–G–J rests on top of body.

6. Coax the trunk to curl upwards and turn up the small flap at end of it.

7. *Tail:* Fringe end of tail. Fold the piece in half, lengthwise, and oversew on the right side L–M.

8. Push scissors right through body piece at centre back as shown on

Fig. 17   Inside of Elephant's body.

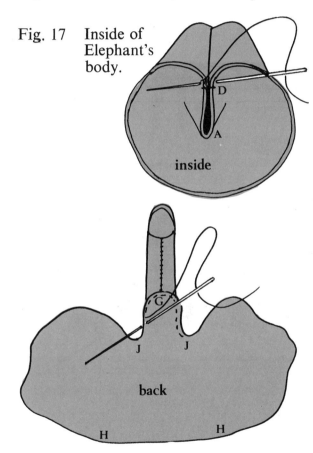

Fig. 18   Making Elephant's head.

pattern to make hole for tail. Push end of tail L right into hole and stitch in place. Coax tail to turn upwards.

"He lieth under the shady trees in the covert of the reed and fens."

(Job 40.21)

A SWINE FROM SQUARES
(or a patchwork pig)

"And the Swine though he divide the hoof and be cloven footed yet he cheweth not the cud; he is unclean to you. Of their flesh shall ye not eat and their carcase ye shall not touch."   (Leviticus 11.7 and 8)

It is said that the ancient Hebrews detested this animal so much that they would not pronounce its name but called it "that beast" or "that thing"—which is probably why even today we call someone we consider low and mean a swine.

This pig is not at all detestable. He is completely washable and made entirely in patchwork, which is appropriate because it is thought that patchwork was widely used for clothes in biblical times, particularly by the Egyptians.

YOU WILL NEED

Odd scraps of cotton material in shades of pink.
Three or four postcards.
Black stranded embroidery cotton.
A piece of foam rubber 4 × 6 inches × 1 inch thick (10 × 15 × 2·5 cm) (Woolworth's). (Or several thicknesses built up to make one inch.)

HOW TO MAKE HIM

1. Cut 68 1-inch (2·5-cm) squares from the postcard and cover each one with cotton material (Fig. 19 A, B, C, D, E).

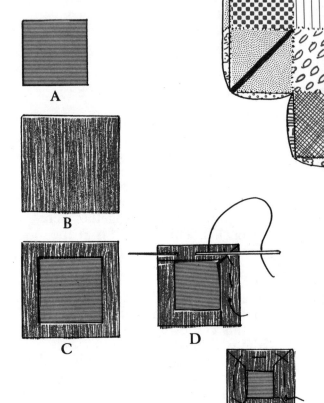

Fig. 19   Preparing a patch.

2. On the wrong side oversew 21 of these together to make one side of pig (Fig. 20 A). Follow picture for positions. The easiest way is to sew them in strips (Fig. 20 B), then sew each strip together.

3. Make the other side in the same way, remembering to reverse it so as to have snout at other end.

4. Sew 22 of the remaining patches together in a long continuous strip and join in a ring.

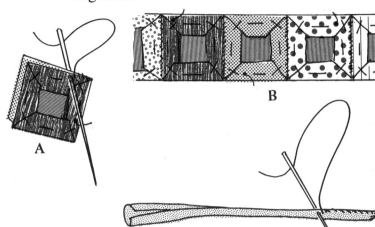

Fig. 20 Oversewing the patches together.

Fig. 22 Making Swine's tail.

5. Starting at tail end, oversew one edge of strip to one side of pig, matching squares. Then sew other edge of strip to other side of pig except for the five squares along top of back.

6. Remove all tackings and cards. Turn pig right side.

7. *Filling:* Using old scissors cut foam rubber to shape and size of pig and slip inside, pushing legs and snout carefully into place.

8. Neatly oversew top opening, matching squares.

9. *Ears:* On the wrong side oversew the remaining four patches together in pairs, working all round three sides (Fig. 21 A). Remove tacking and cards (B), turn right side out, push out corners with tips of

scissors (C), turn in and oversew opening. Fold and stitch in place for ears.

10. *Tail:* Cut a strip of material $4 \times \frac{1}{2}$ inches (10×1.5 cm). Turn long edges inwards and oversew, also ends (Fig. 22). Sew to pig. Curl round as picture and catch in this position.

11. Embroider eye and mouth with black cotton.

"As a jewel of gold in a swine's snout so is a fair woman which is without discretion." (Proverbs 11.22)

In other words Jewish and Arabian women often wore rings in their noses to make themselves beautiful but a jewel in a swine's snout is just as ridiculous, useless and meaningless as a beautiful woman who has no discretion.

It seems probable that the Hebrews' loathing of swine was so great that they bred few or no pigs at all in those early days, but of course by New Testament times there were many herds of swine.

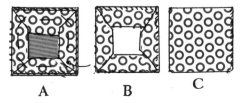

A　　　B　　　C

Fig. 21 Making Swine's ears.

'Can the leopard change his spots?' (Jeremiah 13.23)

In this working model—yes, he can, and you will have fun doing it! However we are told in Jeremiah that it was just as impossible to reform those Jews who had by their wicked ways become accustomed to sinning, as to change a leopard's spots.

YOU WILL NEED

Two pieces of thick cardboard $2 \times 9\frac{3}{4}$ inches (5 × 25 cm).
Two pieces of thin white cardboard the size of this page and one strip 13 × 3 inches (33 × 7·5 cm).

HOW TO MAKE THE MODEL

1. Trace the leopard from page 88 on to one piece of thin card.

2. Cut out all the outlined holes shown on the pattern shape, using small pointed scissors and working very carefully. (These are some of his spots.)

3. Paint the leopard yellow. When dry, paint his claws, face and a lot more spots in black. (Look at the picture.) Do not touch the holes you have cut out.

4. Paint the strip of thin card with $\frac{1}{2}$-inch (1·5-cm) wide yellow and black stripes on one side.

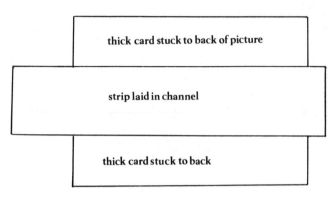

Fig. 23   Making a "channel" at back of model.

5. Turn the picture over. Stick the two pieces of thick cardboard to the back of the picture, one along top and one along bottom, thus making a channel along which the striped strip will slide (Fig. 23).

6. Remove striped strip and stick the second piece of thin card the same size as your picture to the back, attaching it to the two pieces of thick card only and leaving the centre channel free.

7. Slide the striped strip, stripes to the front, into the channel (Fig. 24).

8. As you pull this backwards and forwards the leopard will change some of his spots.

Noah's Ark

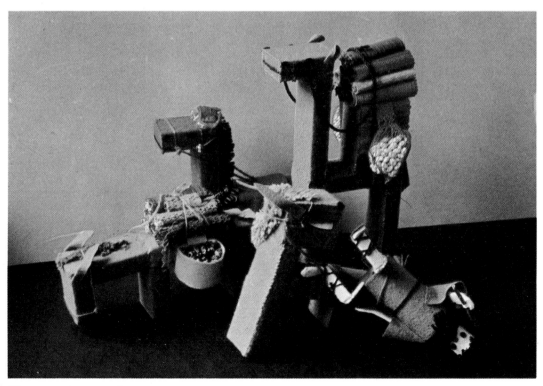

Horses and a camel

Noah and his family

Daniel and the Lion

thin card stuck to back of picture

Fig. 24   Finishing off back.

In those far-off days leopards prowled everywhere and were greatly feared by the shepherds. The Bible makes great use of them as examples of swift, subtle and fierce beasts.

" . . . the spirit of wisdom and understanding . . . shall rest upon him . . . and the wolf also shall dwell with the lamb and the leopard shall lie down with the kid . . ."

(Isaiah 11.2 and 6)

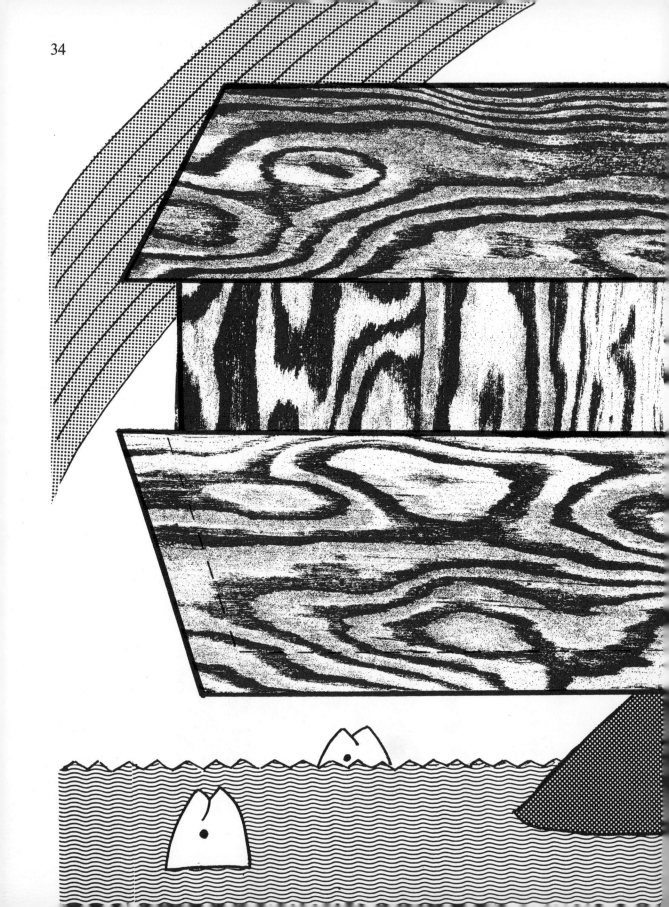

NOAH'S ARK
as a pocket picture

" . . . God said unto Noah . . .
make thee an ark of gopher wood
. . . rooms shall thou make in the
ark . . . with lower, second and
third stories shalt thou make it . . ."

" . . . I do bring a flood of waters
upon the earth to destroy all
flesh . . . and everything that is in
the earth shall die . . ."
(Genesis 6.14, 16, 17)

I have made my ark in the form of
a "pocket picture". The Noah
family are finger puppets (page 38)
and the animals are made of wool
and paper over pipe-cleaner frames
(pages 40–45). You can make as
many or as few as you wish and
tuck them all into the pocket on
the ark so that they appear to be
standing on the deck.

We have to remember that in
Noah's day communications with
the outside world were such that
"earth" was merely just as far as
one could travel, and that "every
living thing" were those animals to
be found on that part of the earth.
It was therefore quite possible for
Noah to have built his ark and
gathered his family and all the
wildlife of the neighbourhood into
it. It is thrilling to think that the
clay stratum discovered at Ur in
the "Fertile Crescent" of the Bible
lands shows that there was in fact
an enormous storm and flood in
about 4000 B.C.—a storm very

similar to what is sometimes
experienced today in the Ganges
Delta, the Gulf of Mexico and
Florida, and which we call a
cyclone. It is even more thrilling
to know that explorers and pilots
have several times reported seeing
the prow of an enormous ship
sticking out of a glacier on the
snow-capped summit of Mount
Ararat. Expeditions have constantly
set out to try to find this ship—
can it really be there, and if so is it
the ark? I'd love to know and I
have a feeling that one day we *shall*
find it.

YOU WILL NEED

A piece of strong cardboard about
the size of this book when opened
flat, for a "base".
A piece of sky-blue material large
enough to cover it.
An odd strip of bluey-green material
for the water.
Scrap of grey felt for the top of
Mount Ararat.
White postcard for the dove.
Silver paper or material for the
fish.
Oddments of "wood grain" Fablon
or Con-Tact for the ark and thin
cardboard for "support".
Paper and paint for the rainbow.

HOW TO MAKE IT

1. Cut out the two fish, Mount Ararat, the rainbow, roof and boat of ark, tracing from picture on pages 34 and 35 (which is actual size). The side of the ark in wood grain Fablon or Con-Tact (a piece $11\frac{1}{2} \times 2$ inches) (22×5 cm). A card support for boat of ark (shown by broken line on picture) and the dove (pattern page 92) (11 pieces in all).

2. Cover the board tightly with the sky blue material by lacing across the back (see page 7, Fig. 1).

3. *Water:* Cut a strip of greeny blue material for the water. "Pink" across one long side and stick or glue to bottom of board. Turn the ends and lower edge back behind the board and stick firmly in place.

4. *Fish:* Stick on the fish. Ink in their eyes and mouths.

5. *Ararat:* Stick the top of Mount Ararat in the centre, rising out of the water.

6. *Rainbow:* Paint the rainbow in stripes of red, orange, yellow, green, blue, indigo and violet, in that order starting from the outer curve, and stick it in place.

"I do set my bow in the cloud and it shall be for a token of a covenant between me and the earth . . . the waters shall no more become a flood to destroy all flesh . . ."
(Genesis 9.13, 15)

7. *The Ark:* Looking at the picture, stick side of Ark in place, then the roof.

8. Stick the card "support" to the back of the boat part, thus leaving $\frac{1}{2}$–$\frac{3}{4}$ inch ($1 \cdot 5$–2 cm) all round the sides and base without a card backing. Stick the boat in place, attaching the sides and lower edge (the unbacked strip) only, thus making a "pocket". You may find that the Fablon's own adhesive backing is all that is needed to stick the three ark pieces in place, or you may find that it will not adhere to your background material, in which case use Copydex or Elmer's Glue-All.

9. *The Dove:* On both sides, ink feathers and eye, and paint beak orange. Cut slit in tail and wings and two on body as marked on pattern. Slip tail into slit B, wings into slit A. Stick one side of one wing and one side of tail end of body and tail to picture so that head end and one wing are loose and stand forward. Stick a scrap of green paper or felt to the beak for the olive branch.

" . . . the dove came to him in the evening; and lo, in her mouth was an olive leaf pluckt off: so Noah knew that the waters were abated from off the earth."   (Genesis 8.11)

THE NOAH FAMILY
as finger puppets

" . . . Noah went in and his sons and his wife and his sons' wives with him into the ark because of the waters of the flood . . ."

(Genesis 7.7)

The Noah family are simply knitted finger puppets—there are five of them so that they conveniently fill one hand!

YOU WILL NEED

Odd scraps of wool any colour and ply for the tunics.
Beige wool for the heads.
An assortment of white, black, brown and grey wool for hair and eyes.
Red stranded embroidery cotton for noses and mouths.
A handful of kapok or cotton wool to stuff heads.
Two knitting needles size 11 or 12 (USA sizes 2 or 1).

HOW TO MAKE THEM

Start with Noah himself.

1. *Tunic:* Cast on 16 stitches. Work 2 rows in K1.P1. rib to stop the edge curling. Work in stocking stitch and stripes of two rows dark and two light for 25 rows. Change to beige wool for head and work in stocking stitch for 15 rows. Break off wool, leaving about 12 inches (30 cm). Thread the end into a

long needle and run this through the stitches, slipping them off the knitting needle. Pull up tightly and fasten off on wrong side, then sew up back seam to form a tube (Fig. 25). Turn right side out.

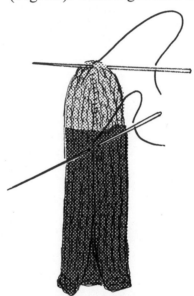

Fig. 25   Sewing up finger puppet.

2. *Head:* Stuff beige head part very firmly, rounding and shaping it as you work. Run a gathering thread all round "neck" (where the striped part joins the beige), pull up very tightly and fasten off by stitching through and through neck several times (Fig. 26).

3. *Hair and Beard:* Sew on a little bundle of white wool for beard and another to top of head for hair as

Mr Noah   **Mrs Noah**   **Shem**   **Ham**   **Japheth**

shown in Fig. 51, page 66, for Jonah. Spread a little adhesive over head, press wool down and arrange neatly. Trim hair and beard.

4. *Features:* Embroider brown eyes, white brows and red nose. (When you put Noah on your finger, the tip will just reach to his neck and his head will stand up above.)

Now make Mrs. Noah, Shem, Ham and Japheth in the same way, varying the colours of their tunics and hair, also their hair styles. A few woollen stitches on the forehead will make a fringe or on the chin a short beard. The picture will help you. When not in use tuck the family into the pocket of the ark, and if you want to make more you can knit a wife each for Shem, Ham and Japheth.

" . . . Noah was six hundred years old when the flood of waters was upon the earth . . ." (Genesis 7.6) —that is why I gave him white hair!

Fig. 26   Making the head.

THE ANIMALS

"Of every clean beast thou shalt take to thee by sevens the male and his female: and of beasts that are not clean by two, the male and his female . . . to keep seed alive upon the face of all the earth."

(Genesis 7.2, 3)

Although it is obvious that Noah could not possibly have taken every living thing into the ark but only those within a reasonable distance, we always imagine him with an ark full of every animal we can think of. I'm sure he *did* take camels, lions and leopards but probably not zebras or giraffes! However, we'll make them just the same.

FOR EACH ANIMAL YOU WILL NEED

Pipe cleaners.
Soft toilet paper.
Wool of the correct colour.
Paint for spots and stripes.

GIRAFFE (7 pipe cleaners and 2 small odd pieces). (Fig. 27).

1. *Frame:* Twist 3 pairs of cleaners together as shown for the sheep, page 25, Fig. 15 (A), making 3 thick pieces, and bend to a U shape (B), one for each pair of legs.

2. Bend the top $\frac{3}{4}$ inch (2 cm) of one pair forwards—these are the hindlegs (A), which need to be shorter to give the giraffe a sloping body.

3. Bend the third pair for the body —$\frac{3}{4}$ inch (2 cm) at top for head (C), $2\frac{1}{4}$ inches (5·5 cm) downwards for neck (D). N.B. this piece is shown in yellow for clarity.

4. Slip this bent body piece between the two pairs of legs, having the forelegs resting in the bend at end of neck at D and making the final body about $1\frac{1}{2}$ inches (4 cm) long. Twist the body piece back over itself and wrap it round and round the top of hindlegs, E, F.

5. Secure forelegs by twisting the seventh pipe cleaner round between them and body (shown in black for clarity and drawn loosely on G). Twist all together firmly and tightly and squeeze together.

6. *Padding out:* Cut $\frac{1}{2}$-inch wide (1·5 cm) strips from a roll of soft crepe toilet paper and bind the framework as shown in H to shape and pad out where necessary. Stick ends of paper to secure. As you bind include two "ends" of pipe cleaners to stick up one each side of top of head for "horns".

7. *Finishing off:* Bind giraffe tightly all over with yellow wool (I) as shown for monkey, page 42, Fig. G. Make a tail by doubling three 4-inch (10-cm) lengths of wool, making 6 "ends" and binding the top half (J). Sew in place, working through top loops. Take a row of loose "oversewing" stitches in brown wool all down back of neck for mane. Snip off "horns",

Fig. 27   Construction of Giraffe.

making them very short. Paint these and the nose and four hoofs black and paint black or brown patches on body.

When you have finished the giraffe try making a horse in the same way but with shorter legs and neck.

Then try a zebra—binding the frame with white wool and painting on the black stripes afterwards.

MONKEY (4 pipe cleaners). (Fig. 28).

1. *Frame:* Fold one cleaner in half and bend into U shape (A). Twist together making a doubled piece (B), then bend this to U shape for front legs (C).

2. Fold two more pipe cleaners in half and twist together as (A–B), one for *each* hind leg. Join them by twisting together at top (D).

3. Leaving a single thickness 2 inches (5 cm) long protruding for tail, twist the fourth cleaner round between top of hind legs and leaving one inch (2·5 cm) between the two pairs of legs for body, twist it between top arch of front legs and wind backwards and forwards round itself. E shows this fourth pipe cleaner loosely in position and coloured for clarity. Bind and twist them all firmly and tightly together. Bend and adjust framework to shape, F.

4. Bind frame all over with brown wool, winding several times over the body and "shoulders" to fatten them a little, thread end into needle and fasten off with a few stitches taken right through the monkey. Take a few stitches over front on each "hand" and foot and tip of tail to cover ends of cleaners, G, and if the white cleaner persists in showing through, dab a little black ink on it to darken.

5. *Head:* Make a tiny ball from crumpled paper and brown wool as shown for the owl page 46, Fig. 31—just as small as your fingers will allow—and sew securely to monkey's shoulders. There is no need to add features. Adjust for firm standing.

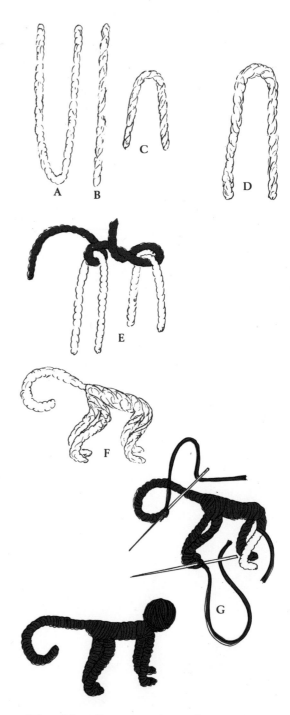

Fig. 28   Construction of Monkey.

CAMEL (6 pipe cleaners). (Fig. 29).

1. *Frame:* Twist 3 pairs of pipe cleaners together as shown for the sheep, page 25, Fig. 15, making three pieces.

2. Bend one pair as A for hind legs and one as B for front legs.

3. Take the third pair and bend ½ inch (1·5 cm) forward for head, curve the next 1¾ inches (4·5 cm) for neck.

4. Slip this piece C between the front legs and twist round to secure them, then through back legs and twist back round and round body— this third piece is shown loosely in position and in colour for clarity, but it should be squeezed and twisted tightly together, leaving about 1½ inches (4 cm) between the two pairs of legs (D).

5. *Padding out:* Cut ½-inch (1·5-cm) strips from a roll of soft crepe toilet paper and bind the framework as shown in E to pad out and shape where necessary. Stick ends of paper to secure.

6. *Hump:* Make a little ball as given for the owl, page 46, Fig. 31, using camel-coloured wool, and sew in place for hump (E). This should reach almost level with top of head.

7. *Finishing off:* (F) Bind carefully and tightly all over with camel-coloured wool, occasionally threading the end into a needle and stitching backwards and forwards through body to secure. Cover "toes" by stitching. Make two little loops of wool for ears. Make the

tail and attach it exactly as given for giraffe, Fig. 27 J, but use two doubled strands of wool only and make it 1¼ inches (3 cm) long. Embroider black eyes.

Fig. 29   Construction of Camel.

44

LION (5 pipe cleaners). (Fig. 30).

1. *Frame:* Twist two pairs of pipe cleaners together as shown for sheep, page 25, Fig. 15 (A).

2. Bend one pair to shape A for forelegs and one to shape B for hindlegs.

3. Slip the third pipe cleaner between these two (C).

4. Pinch the bent part of the tops of legs together so that D's and E's meet and twist cleaner C back over the pieces and round and round to form a body about $1\frac{3}{4}$ inches (4·5 cm) long. This cleaner is shown coloured and loosely twisted for clarity, but the frame should actually be pinched and twisted tightly together, leaving ends protruding for neck (G).

5. *Padding and shaping:* (H) Cut $\frac{1}{2}$-inch (1·5-cm) wide strips off a roll of soft crepe toilet paper and bind frame tightly, thickening body, neck and top of legs.

6. *Binding:* (I) Bind lion all over with tawny-coloured wool, threading the end into a needle now and then and stitching through the body several times to secure. "Oversew" toes and top of neck with matching wool to secure leg bindings and cover ends of cleaners.

7. *Head and Tail:* (J) Make a tiny ball about $\frac{3}{4}$ inch (2 cm) diameter of matching wool as given for the owl, page 46, Fig. 31, and sew to top of neck for head. Make tail as given for giraffe (Fig. 27 J), but use two doubled strands of wool only and make it $1\frac{1}{2}$ inches (4 cm) long, binding almost to end. Sew to lion.

8. *Mane and Face:* (J and K). Take a series of long, looped stitches, working round and round the "face" until they completely frame the face and cover the back of the head. Cut loops and fluff out wool. Embroider black nose and mouth and green eyes.

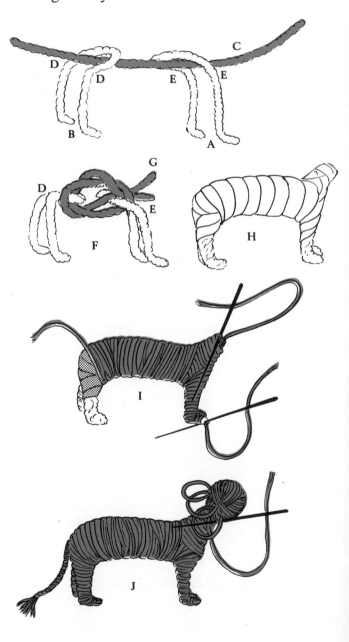

Fig. 30   Construction of Lion.

You can easily convert your lion.

1. To a *lioness* by leaving off the mane and adding small loops of wool for ears.

2. To a *tiger* by leaving off the mane, changing the tail, adding ears and painting black stripes.

3. To a *leopard* by making the body slimmer, leaving off mane, adding ears and painting black spots.

The same face does for them all and is shown front view on the tiger.

You will not be able to get many animals into the pocket of your ark at once, but there is nothing to stop you making a large selection and changing them around from time to time. These ideas should start you experimenting with other creatures.

"And they went in unto Noah into the ark, two and two of all flesh, wherein is the breath of life."
                                    (Genesis 7.15)

A WOOLLY OWL

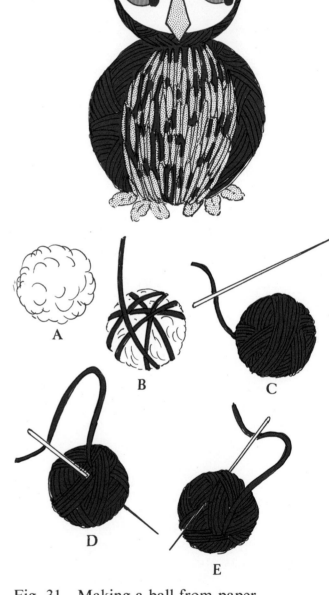

"I will wail and howl . . . I will
make a mourning as the owls."
(Micah 1.8)

What a wonderful description of
the noise some owls make—
"mourning"! I don't think this owl
will wail and howl, he looks much
too cheeky.

YOU WILL NEED

Tissue paper and brown and fawn
wool for head and body.
Scraps of felt: brown for "tufts",
white, green, yellow and black for
features.
Two pipe cleaners and yellow poster
paint for feet.

HOW TO MAKE HIM

1. Cut out the "face", eyes, slits,
beak and tufts (patterns page 86).
(8 pieces).

2. *Head and Body:* Make two balls
from tissue paper and brown wool,
one a little larger than a golf ball
for the head and the second one
half as big again for the body, by
crumpling tissue paper, winding
wool all over to completely cover
and finishing off by stitching several
times through and through the ball.
(Fig. 31, A, B, C, D, E).
(Whilst stitching, make sure you
put your needle through any wool
which seems as though it might
slip, and secure it firmly.)

Fig. 31 Making a ball from paper
and wool.

Fig. 32 Side view of Owl's head.

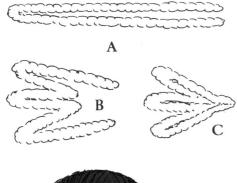

A

B

C

Fig. 33 Owl's feet.

3. *Breast feathers:* Using a long needle and fawn wool, take long, straight stitches over about one quarter of the large ball to represent light-coloured breast feathers.

4. Using a long needle and brown wool sew the two balls securely together, working round and round the neck several times.

5. *Features:* Stick the "tufts" in place, then the white "face", green eyes and black slits.

6. Stick the beak in place, attaching outside edges only and arching it a little so that the point is loose and stands away from the face (Fig. 32).

7. Fold each pipe cleaner as shown in Fig. 33 A. Bend for feet (B and C). Dip into thick yellow paint and when dry sew to base of owl (Fig. 34).

". . . and these are they which ye shall have in abomination among the fowls, they shall not be eaten . . . the owl . . . the little owl . . . and the great owl."

(Leviticus 11.13, 16, 17)

JACOB'S LADDER— a working model

"And he dreamed, and behold, a ladder set on the earth and the top of it reached to heaven and the angels of God ascending and descending on it."   (Genesis 28.12)

Can you imagine this dream? Jacob must have been very sorry to wake up and wished he could go back to sleep and see it all over again.

I have thought of a way to make a sort of ladder which stretches and shrinks so that the angels on it appear to be going up and down. It looks complicated but is really quite easy.

YOU WILL NEED

Some very strong cardboard and 13 fairly short paper fasteners for ladder.
Stiff white paper for angels' dresses.
Four small lightweight buttons about ¾ inch (2 cm) diameter for heads.
Scrap of pale pink material for faces.
A postcard and silver or gold foil for haloes.
Eight white feathers for wings.

HOW TO MAKE IT

1. Cut out rungs of ladder and skirts (patterns page 90). (14 pieces).

Jonah and the Whale

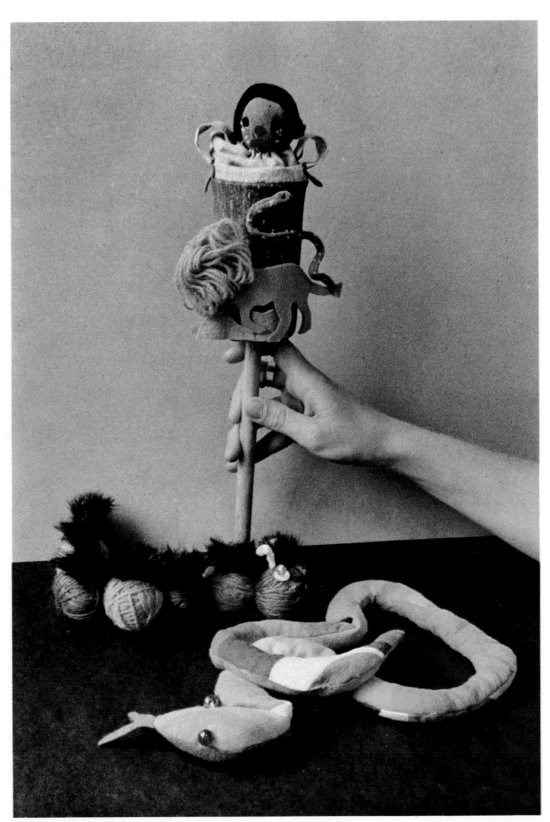

Serpent, caterpillar and emerging Joseph

2. *Dresses:* Roll the paper dresses round to make a cone so that the A's match and the flap A–B tucks underneath. Stick in place.

3. *Faces:* Cover the buttons with a larger circle of pink material, gathering round edge, pulling up gathers and fastening off at back (Fig. 34 A and B).

4. *Haloes:* Cut four circles of postcard about 1¼ inches (3·5 cm) diameter. Wrap in silver or gold foil (or cut from silver or gold card if you have it).

5. Use some very strong adhesive to stick faces to tops of dresses, then halo to back of each dress and face and two white feathers to back of dress and halo for wings (Fig. 35).

6. With ballpoint pen mark blue eyes and red nose and mouth.

7. Stick a short piece of thick yellow wool round top of face for hair.

8. *Ladder:* The cardboard used must be strong or your finished ladder will bend. If you have difficulty in cutting it use a thinner card and *after* cutting stick two thicknesses together. Following picture pierce holes in each strip, two each in the long and short pieces and three in the medium pieces. (A needlework stiletto is ideal for this if you have one.) Fasten the pieces loosely together with paper fasteners, two long pieces at the bottom for handles and the two shortest at the top to finish off. Make sure you have all the pieces sloping to the right on top and all those to the left underneath or vice versa. Test

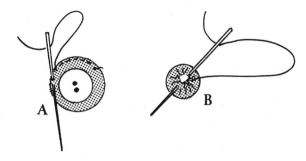

Fig. 34   Making Angel's face.

Fig. 35   Back view of Angel.

by taking a handle in each hand and pulling them gently first together then apart—the ladder should grow and shrink. If your paper fasteners are too long, cut off surplus ends with old scissors or wire cutters.

9. Stick the angels firmly here and there on the ladder, making sure you place them so as not to interfere with its working.

" . . . and Jacob awakened out of his sleep . . . and said . . . this is the gate of heaven . . ."

(Genesis 28.16, 17)

A LONG-HAIRED GOAT

" . . . thou art fair, my love; . . .
thy hair is as a flock of goats . . ."
                    (Song of Solomon 4.1)

This goat has long, straight "hair",
otherwise is very similar to the
sheep on page 24.

YOU WILL NEED

Approximately 19 pipe cleaners for
the hair.
A small piece of very strong, white
cardboard for the body.
Black ink.

HOW TO MAKE HIM

1. Cut out the body (pattern page
96). (1 piece).

2. Draw mouth, nostrils and eyes
on both sides, copying from
pattern.

3. *Legs:* Make exactly as for sheep
(page 24, no. 4, Fig. 15, A, B, C
and D).

4. *Horns:* Push one pipe cleaner
through hole and press flat and
upwards—half on each side of card
(Fig. 36, A1). Fold each half down
on to itself (B1). Press tightly
together and curve backwards (C1).

5. *Beard:* Push half a pipe cleaner
through hole so that half of the
piece is on each side of card (Fig.
36, A2). Fold each piece in half
upwards and press flat (B2). Arrange
each side to completely cover
cardboard shape of beard (C2).

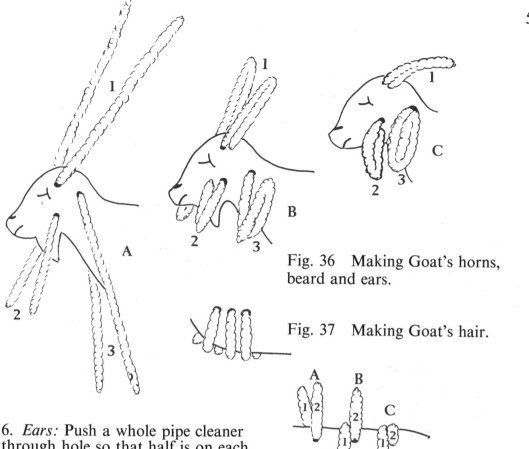

Fig. 36   Making Goat's horns, beard and ears.

Fig. 37   Making Goat's hair.

Fig. 38   Covering top edge of back.

6. *Ears:* Push a whole pipe cleaner through hole so that half is on each side of card (Fig. 36 A3). Fold each half up and down (B3). Press flat to make a long, slim ear on each side of head (C3).

7. *Tail:* Work as for beard, using the other half of that cleaner. Press flat and curl backwards.

8. *Hair:* Make a series of holes (about 27) on top half of body only. Cut 12 pipe cleaners into 3. Start at lower holes and thread these pieces through, folding them flat down against card on each side so that the cut ends just cover lower edge of card (Fig. 37).

9. Continue in this way, working upwards so that the whole body becomes covered with "hair", until you come to the top row of holes. When pushing pipe cleaner pieces

through these, bend them upwards (Fig. 38 A). Cross each piece over and bring the end down on opposite side of top of back (B and C), thus covering top cardboard edge. Add more holes and pipe cleaners wherever necessary.

10. With a small paintbrush and black drawing ink paint the horns, ears and "hoofs" black and touch pipe cleaners here and there all over body to give depth and shade to the hair. When dry, adjust your goat to stand firmly.

"... all the spotted and speckled among the goats ..."

(Genesis 30.32)

DANIEL AND THE LION
—as hand puppets

" . . . He hath shut the lions'
mouths that they have not hurt
me . . ." (Daniel 6.22)

Although the lions were obviously very kind-hearted, I'm sure Daniel was extremely frightened when he was thrown into their den—so I have made two puppets—one for each hand, a rather scared Daniel and a soft, happy lion. Your thumbs and little fingers slip through openings in the body and form the "arms" of the puppets as this gives greater flexibility in working them. In the case of the lion, knitted tubes, like the fingers of a glove, are worn.

YOU WILL NEED

An empty tube from a toilet roll to line heads.
Tissue paper and thin rag for padding head.
Piece of an old pair of tights for Daniel's head.
Oddment of firm material for Daniel's tunic.
Oddments of tawny, lion-coloured material for lion.
A few yards of matching double knitting wool for arms.
Scraps of black, white and red felt for eyes, tongue, mouth and hair.

HOW TO MAKE DANIEL

1. Cut out tunic, hair, beard, eyes, pupils, mouth and eyebrows (patterns pages 94: 95: 96) (12 pieces).

2. Cut the tube in half and put one piece away for the lion. Bind edge with Scotch tape to stop it "unrolling" (Fig. 39 A).

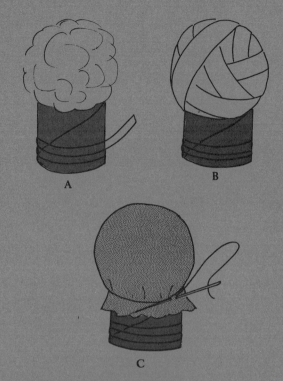

Fig. 39   Making puppet's head.

3. *Head:* Crumple tissue paper into a tight knob making a ball about 2 inches (5 cm) across over one end of the tube (Fig. 39 A). Bind round and over this with narrow strips of thin rag. Secure ends with adhesive (B).

4. Pull a double thickness of the top of a pair of old tights over the "ball". Gather all round "neck", pull up, stitch and fasten off firmly (C).

5. *Tunic:* On the wrong side stick or stitch side seams of tunic and a narrow turning all round "sleeve" edge and neck. Pink bottom or turn up a narrow hem.

6. Turn right side out. Stick tunic all round "neck", covering head gathers, putting the back on first,

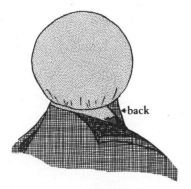

Fig. 40   Joining head and tunic.

then overlapping front at "shoulders" (Fig. 40).

7. *Nose:* Make a little "knob" about the size of a pea by gathering up a tiny circle of the double tights material to match the face and stuffing with cotton wool. (Like the faces of angels, page 49, no. 3, Fig. 34 A and B, but use cotton wool instead of a button.) Stick to face, also eyebrows, eyes, pupils and mouth.

8. *Hair:* Fringe beard and hair pieces as shown on pattern. Stick on hair piece A, short fringe to front, then beard, then hair piece B across top of head, pressing well down all over. Trim if necessary.

9. To use your puppet put your thumb through one side slit, your little finger through the other and your middle three fingers in the tube.

"Whatsoever thy hand findeth to do, do it with thy might!"
(Ecclesiastes 9.10)

HOW TO MAKE THE LION

1. Cut out the body, pupils, eyes, nose, mouth, tongue, ears and ear linings (patterns pages 94, 95). (13 pieces).

2, 3, 4, 5 and 6. Work exactly as for Daniel but use material to match body for head instead of tights.

7. *Face:* Cut a circle of card the size of top of a small beaker (approximately $3\frac{1}{2}$ inches or 8·5 cm) and two circles the size of a coffee saucer ($4\frac{1}{2}$–5 inches or 11–12 cm) in material to match body.

8. Stick these three pieces together with the small card circle between the larger material circles, but only put adhesive on the *card* so that the overhanging edges of material are not joined (Fig. 41). Fringe all round from edge of material circles to card to make mane, snipping each of the two layers separately so that the cuts come in different places.

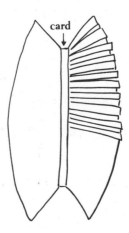

Fig. 41   Making Lion's face and mane.

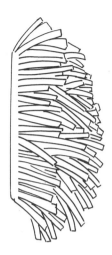

Fig. 42   Side view of Lion's head.

9. Stick on ears, ear linings, eyes, pupils, nose, mouth and tongue.

10. Press head to flatten the front as much as possible and stick face securely in place.

11. Cut one or two small rectangles of material, fringe them and stick here and there over back of head to cover it and continue mane (Fig. 42)

12. *"Arms":* With size 12 (USA: 1) knitting needles and matching "tawny" wool, cast on 15 stitches and work 1 row K.1 P.1 rib to stop the ends curling. Work in stocking stitch for 26 rows. Break off wool leaving about 12 inches (30 cm). Thread this end into long needle and run it through the stitches, slipping them off the needle. Pull up and fasten off on wrong side, then sew up seam to form a "tube". Make another in the same way and wear these on your thumb and little finger when using your lion, arranging the seams down the back where they don't show.

" . . . so Daniel was taken up out of the den and no manner of hurt was found upon him . . ."

(Daniel 6.23)

THE SPIDER AND HER WEB

"There be . . . things which are little upon the earth but they are exceeding wise . . . the spider taketh hold with her hands and is in kings' palaces."

(Proverbs 30.24 and 28)

FOR THE SPIDER YOU WILL NEED

2 pipe cleaners and some black ink for legs.
2 green sequins for eyes.
A piece of tissue paper for body.
A few yards of black wool.

HOW TO MAKE HER

1. Make two balls with tissue paper and black wool as shown for the owl on page 46, no. 2 and Fig. 31, A, B, C, D and E—one about the size of a walnut for the body and one about one third of the size for the head.

2. Sew the two together and sew on the sequin eyes.

3. Cut the pipe cleaners in half and sew the four pieces to underside in the join between head and body.

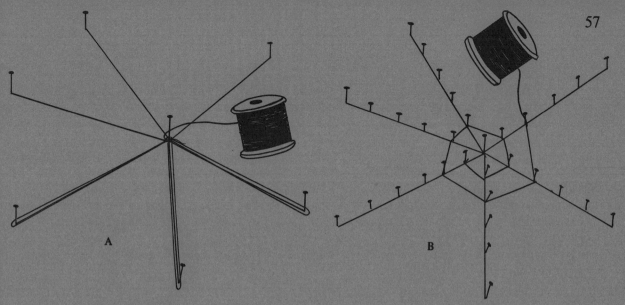

Fig. 43   Making the Spider's web.

4. Spread the legs out and bend to shape. Paint them all over with black ink, stand the spider on an old newspaper and put away to dry. You can hang her up by a thread if you like.

FOR THE WEB YOU WILL NEED

A reel of white cotton.
Hair lacquer.
A lot of pins.
An old piece of cardboard to work on.

HOW TO MAKE IT

1. Roughly draw a spider's web on the cardboard. (N.B. Figs. 43 A and B do not show this drawing, to avoid confusion.)

2. Push a pin into every corner.

3. Tie the end of the cotton to centre pin and first make the cross pieces, winding the cotton out round one pin back to the centre, then out round the next and back and so on until all the crosspieces (which will be double) are made. Do not break off cotton (Fig. A).

4. Now "spin" the web, working round and round each "circle" of pins from centre outwards. Fasten off cotton at last pin in outside ring (Fig. B).

5. Spray the web thoroughly with hair lacquer. Allow to dry, then repeat the process.

6. Pull out pins and carefully lift web off card, putting a tiny spot of colourless nail varnish or glue at each "join" if it seems to need it.

You will find this quite strong— very different from the wonderful example of frailty given by Bildad.

" . . . the hypocrite's hope shall perish, it shall be cut off and his trust shall be as the spider's web."
(Job 8.13, 14)

Joseph struggles to get out of the pit—a pop-up toy

" . . . they stript Joseph out of his coat of many colours . . . and they took him and cast him into a pit . . . we will say some evil beast hath devoured him . . ."

(Genesis 37.23, 24, 20)

Poor Joseph must have hated this and I can imagine him struggling to get out, so in this model he is crying! Of course his "coat of many colours" was really a beautiful long tunic with long sleeves like those worn by noblemen, probably in red or purple, whilst his jealous brothers wore a short, sleeveless tunic of rough material.

YOU WILL NEED

One empty ½ pint cream or yoghurt carton for the pit.
A piece of cane or dowelling about ½ inch thick × 14 inches long (1·5 × 35 cm).
Rough brown material to cover carton.
Oddment of neutral material for Joseph's garment. (He has been "stript" of his coat of many colours.)
Piece of the top of old pair of tights and cotton wool for head.
Black wool for hair. Tawny wool for lion's mane.
Crystal beads for tears.
Scraps of felt: red for mouth and nose, black for eyes, fawn for hands, tawny for lion, grey for boulders, green for serpent and grass.
One pipe cleaner for serpent.

HOW TO MAKE THE MODEL

1. Cut out the hands, eyes, nose, mouth (patterns page 93), also two lions in felt and one in postcard as given for "The Creation" (trace from the picture on pages 8 and 9). (9 pieces).

2. *Pit:* Burn a hole in the base of plastic carton with a red-hot poker or the point of an iron, large enough to allow the cane to pass easily through it. (A grown-up should help with this, or alternatively the hole should be cut, but this is more difficult.)

3. Cover carton with rough brown material (furnishing fabric?), sticking seam at back and turning over and sticking inside top of pit (Fig. 44 A).

4. Turn in bottom edge, gather all round and pull up so that the gathers just surround hole (Fig. 44 B).

5. Drill a hole ½ inch (1·5 cm) from one end of cane (Fig. 44 C).

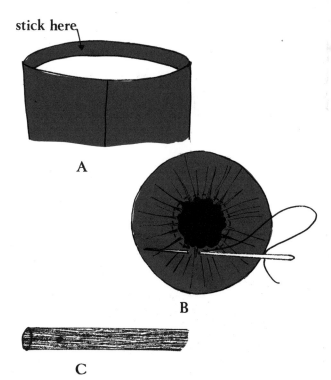

stick here

A

B

C

Fig. 44   Preparing the Pit.

6. *Head:* Make a little "ball" about the size of a golf ball from a double circle cut from the top of an old pair of tights gathered all round the edge and pulled up over a stuffing of cotton wool (or tightly crumpled tissue paper). Push cane into centre, pull up gathers and stitch firmly backwards and forwards through the hole to "anchor" head firmly. Fig. 39 will be a help, but of course this head will be mounted on a slender neck of cane instead of a toilet roll tube.

7. *Tunic:* Cut a piece of drab-coloured material for Joseph's garment, about 4 inches (10 cm) wide and long enough to fit round the top of carton plus seam allowance.

8. Stitch or stick seam on wrong side.

9. Placing seam on garment to that on pit (centre back), pull garment on to pit inside out and oversew bottom of garment (having turned back a narrow hem) to top of carton on the wrong side (Fig. 45).

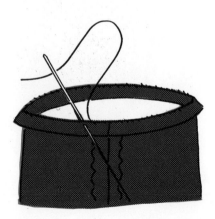

Fig. 45   Joining garment to Pit.

10. Pull garment upwards so that it is right side out. Turn in top $\frac{1}{2}$ inch (1·5 cm), gather all round, push the cane down through garment, carton and out through hole in base, pull up gathers and secure firmly all round the "neck".

11. Make two sleeves $2\frac{1}{4} \times \frac{3}{4}$ inches (6×2 cm) when finished by cutting pieces of material to match tunic, folding in half and turning in and sticking raw edges. Sew hands to one end.

12. Sew top of sleeve to garment about $\frac{3}{4}$ inch (2 cm) from neck and attach wrist lower down about $\frac{1}{2}$ inch (1·5 cm) from top of pit, leaving hands free. (Thumbs forwards.) Page 58, position 3.

13. Try your model by pushing cane "handle" up and down. Joseph should now disappear completely into pit with only two hands showing, (position 1), slowly emerge, his hands turning downwards (position 2), then pop right out, his hands appearing to press on top of pit (position 3).

14. *Hair:* Cover top, sides and back of head with adhesive and press a small bundle of black wool on to it, arranging carefully and trimming ends.

15. *Features:* Stick on eyes, nose and mouth and sew on crystal bead tears.

16. *Lion:* Stick the two felt lion pieces one each side of the card lion. Wind a bundle of matching wool round your three middle fingers (Fig. 46). Slip off and stick to one side of head for mane. Repeat on other side of head.

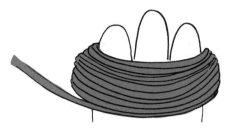

Fig. 46   Making the Lion's mane.

I enjoyed making this, did you?
But it is nice to know that the
story although a long, exciting one
eventually had a happy ending.

" . . . and they drew and lifted up
Joseph out of the pit and sold him
for twenty pieces of silver . . . and
they brought Joseph into Egypt."
(Genesis 37.28)

17. Stick to front of pit. Add one
or two grey boulders and if you
like, stick long felt "grass" round
back of pit.

As for his brothers—perhaps we
ought to remember "He that
diggeth a pit shall fall into it"!
(Ecclesiastes 10.8)

18. *Serpent:* Cover a pipe cleaner
with green felt, stab-stitching all
along one side and shaping off at
ends for head and tail (Fig. 47).
Embroider a black eye and bright
coloured spots. Curl and bend this
and stick here and there to pit,
leaving head and tail free.

Fig. 47   Making the Serpent.

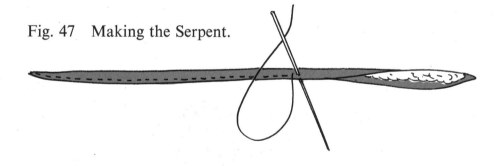

A HORSE from matchboxes

" . . . Harness the horses and get up, ye horsemen . . ."   (Jeremiah 46.4)

Horses were mostly used for war. They were either harnessed to chariots or carried soldiers on their backs and must have been enormous, fearless beasts. To make this one

YOU WILL NEED

6 empty matchboxes.
Brown felt to cover them and scraps for mane and tail.
Bright felt for saddle.
Wool for bridle and reins.
Beads for decoration.

HOW TO MAKE HIM

1. Cut out eyes and nostrils as given for ass, and saddle and ear patterns, all on page 87, also a piece of brown felt 4 × 1 inches (10 × 2·5 cm) for mane and a piece 2½ × 2 inches (6 × 5 cm) for tail. (9 pieces).

2. *Mane:* Fold the mane in half, lengthwise, stab stitch all along fold, then fringe (Fig. 48).

3. *Tail:* Fringe tail piece along one 2½ inch (5 cm) side leaving ½ inch (1·5 cm) "solid" at top. Roll solid end up tightly and secure by stitching. (Look at picture.)

Now make up your horse exactly as given for camel on pages 21/22

nos. 2, 3, 4, 5, 6 and 7 but look at picture for different number and position of matchboxes. Fold ears as for donkey, page 22 (Fig. 13), and sew on mane and tail.

Decorate your horse with gay beads, and if you like make him a "collar" from braid, beads and a few brass headed paper fasteners.

Solomon was the first King to go in for horses in a really big way. He " . . . had forty thousand stalls of horses for his chariots and twelve thousand horsemen . . . barley also and straw for the horses . . ." (1 Kings 4.26 and 28). Just imagine how much food he needed for them all!

Fig. 48 - Making Horse's mane.

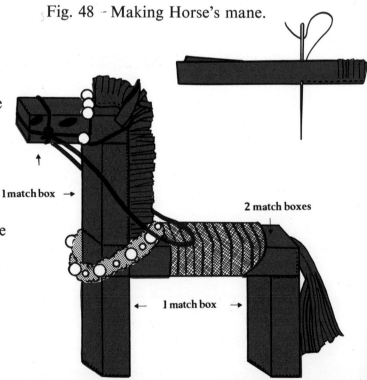

1 match box →

2 match boxes

← 1 match box →

A brown paper moth

" . . . Fear ye not the reproach of men, neither be ye afraid of their revilings. For the moth shall eat them up like a garment and the worm shall eat them like wool . . ."
(Isaiah 51.7, 8)

A grim warning indeed of an untimely end for the wicked! This moth is very placid and I don't think he'll eat anything so we can safely leave him around the house!

YOU WILL NEED

A scrap of tissue paper and a few yards of brown wool for the body. A short piece of *thin* brown plastic-covered garden wire for the legs. A piece of stiff brown paper for wings (or material if you prefer).

HOW TO MAKE HIM

1. Cut out the wings (pattern page 93). (1 piece).

2. *Body and legs:* Work exactly as given for the locust, page 13, nos. 2, 3, 6 and 7 but using brown wool, altering shape of body to that shown in Fig. 49. and cutting wires of legs as follows:

Piece for hindlegs 5 inches (13 cm).
Middle legs 3¼ inches (8·5 cm).
Forelegs 3¼ inches (8.5 cm).
Feelers 2½ inches (6·5 cm).

Fold them as picture above.

3. *Wings:* Draw markings in black ink on both sides. Fold across broken line and stitch to top of back with brown cotton and a fine needle so as not to tear paper.

Fig. 49   Shape of Moth's body.

" . . . Wilt thou break a leaf driven to and fro and . . . pursue the dry stubble? . . . thou writest bitter things against me . . . thou puttest my feet in stocks . . . and he, as a rotten thing, consumeth, as a garment that is moth-eaten."
(Job 13.25–28)

Poor patient Job—at it again!

AN ANGEL from egg cartons

" . . . thou hast made him a little lower than the angels . . ."

(Psalm 8.5)

When I was a very small girl I remember being asked what I thought an angel was and replying, "A sort of holy, religious fairy." The shrieks of laughter which followed reduced me to tears but I still stick to this explanation for *I* know what I mean! However, the dictionary tells us that the correct description is: "Ministering spirit or divine messenger of an order of spiritual beings superior to man in power and intelligence." It struck me that the modern, transparent plastic egg cartons had an ethereal, fairylike appearance and would make an ideal robe for one of my religious fairies.

YOU WILL NEED

A transparent egg carton for the robe.
Scrap of pink material and a knob of cotton wool for the head.
Yellow wool or stranded cotton for hair.
Gold cardboard for halo (from some kinds of chocolate box?).
Strong white button thread and four two-hole white shirt buttons for stringing up.

HOW TO MAKE HER

1. *Hair:* Cut a small "bunch" of wool or cotton about 10 inches (25 cm) long. Wind each end round a pencil; lay carefully on old newspaper where it will not be disturbed. Spray ends very thoroughly with liquid starch or hair lacquer, or paint with colourless gum. Leave on one side until dry and set, preferably overnight. Slide pencils out and you should have a lovely "wig" with soft rolls at each end.

2. *Face:* Cut a circle of pink material the size of a tea cup. Gather all round edge, stuff with cotton wool, pull up gathers and fasten off. Flatten head, having smooth front for face, gathers at centre back. Mark blue eyes and red mouth with ballpoint pen.

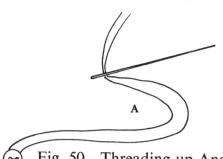

Fig. 50   Threading up Angel's body and wings.

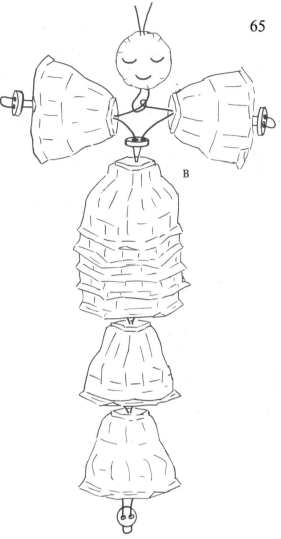

3. *Assembling:* Using old kitchen scissors cut the egg carton up so that you have nine separate cups. Trim edges.

4. Take a long piece of strong, white thread and thread a button on to the *centre*.

5. *Skirt:* Follow Fig. 50. Thread both ends into a long needle so that you have a double thickness and button is at centre (Fig. 50 A).

6. Push needle through middle of base of seven of the plastic "cups", piling one on top of the other to form a skirt.

7. Divide the two strings each on to a separate needle and thread on a button, one string through each hole (Fig. 50 B).

8. *Wings:* On first one needle, then the other, thread first a "cup" then a button, bringing each string through base of cup, one hole of button, back through second hole of button and back through cup (Fig. 50 B). The four buttons will prevent any chance of the strong thread cutting and pulling through the plastic egg carton.

9. Thread both strings into one needle again and pull them through head. Arrange cups and head carefully and tie threads several times to secure at the right tension.

10. *Halo:* Cut a circle of gold card, using an upturned coffee cup as a pattern, and try it behind head for best position. Push needle containing both strings through it, then secure halo to back of head with adhesive covering gathers. Fix strings to back of halo with Sellotape or Scotch tape. Cut ends and make a loop to hang up by.

11. Stick the prepared "hair" to top of head.

You might like to use this angel with Balaam and his ass.

" . . . the angel did wondrously . . ."
(Judges 13.19)

JONAH AND THE WHALE
—a pocket panel

"And Jonah was in the belly of the fish three days and three nights."

(Jonah 1.17)

What a horrid thought—but what a lovely story to use for making a "pocket" panel. Jonah can be sailing along in his boat—fall into the sea, then be swallowed up by the "fish"—which we know as a whale.

YOU WILL NEED

A piece of bright blue felt for the sea 6 × 18 inches (15 × 46 cm) and some matching oddments for waves.
Two discarded knitting needles 6½ inches (16 cm) long.
Scraps of black felt for whale.
Scrap of brown felt for boat.
Scrap of white felt for eye, teeth, sail and crests of waves.
Scrap of flesh pink felt for Jonah.
Grey wool for hair.
Scrap of rough texture, bright material for tunic.
Cocktail stick for mast.
White stranded embroidery cotton for whale's "spout".

HOW TO MAKE IT

1. Cut out the sail, Jonah, boat, whale and teeth (patterns page 90). (6 pieces).

2. *Jonah:* Oversew the two pieces together all round except for opening. With a cocktail stick stuff carefully with a little cotton wool or kapok. Sew up opening.

3. Sew a scrap of material round body across one shoulder for a tunic, fringe round bottom edge (Fig. 51 A).

4. Embroider eyes in black. Sew on a little bundle of fine, grey darning wool for beard (B) and another bundle to top of head for hair (C). Secure beard and hair neatly in place all round with a little adhesive and trim ends (D).

Fig. 51   Making Jonah.

5. Attach a piece of fine cord to top of head (long enough to reach from top to bottom of panel—D).

6. Roll each end of the blue "sea" round a knitting needle. Stab stitch these in place to weight the panel at each end. Finish the ends of needles with a carefully rounded knob of sealing wax. Sew a curtain ring to top end for hanging up, and attach the free end of Jonah's "cord".

7. Look at picture and mentally divide your panel into three.

" . . . he found a ship going to Tarshish . . . he paid the fare thereof and went down into it . . ."
(Jonah 1.3)

" . . . and there was a mighty tempest in the sea so that the ship was like to be broken . . . so they took up Jonah and cast him forth into the sea." (Jonah 1.4, 15)

" . . . the Lord had prepared a great fish to swallow up Jonah.'
(Jonah 1.7)

8. Stick boat and sail in place on top section. Sew on cocktail stick mast and take a few long stitches in strong thread for "rigging".

9. Embroider the "spout" in white cotton on the centre section and stick a tiny "mound" of black felt to the base of it. (This is the tip of whale's snout which will just show above waves.)

10. Stick teeth to *back* of lower jaw of whale so that only the jagged edge shows. Stick on eye and sew a tiny black bead in place for pupil. Stick the completed whale in place to bottom section.

11. Stick white crests and blue waves in place on all three sections, using the picture as a guide.

12. Cut three slits where marked on panel and try Jonah into each one. His position is marked by broken lines on the lower two panels—he will swim in the sea, then be swallowed by the whale.

Of course the story had a happy ending because " . . . the Lord spoke unto the fish and it vomited out Jonah upon the dry land."
(Jonah 2.10)
The adventure seems to have done him good because he behaved much better after it!

BALAAM AND HIS ASS
that sits or stands

" . . . the ass thrust herself unto the wall and crushed Balaam's foot against the wall and he smote her again . . ."   (Numbers 22.25)

" . . . the ass fell down under Balaam and Balaam's anger was kindled and he smote the ass with a staff. And the Lord opened the mouth of the ass and she said unto Balaam 'What have I done unto thee that thou hast smitten me these three times?' " (Numbers 22.27, 28)

And so the second animal in history spoke! The first was the serpent who spoke to Eve. This toy is fun to play with as the ass can carry Balaam on her back riding either astride or side saddle, then sit down and tip him off.

FOR THE ASS YOU WILL NEED

6 empty matchboxes and the tray part of 2.
Sufficient grey felt to cover them.
Scraps of black felt for eyes and nostrils.
$\frac{1}{2}$ pipe cleaner for tail.
Grey fur or fringe for mane.
A white postcard for teeth.
Scrap of bright material for saddle cloth.
Bright wool for reins.

HOW TO MAKE HER

Cut out eyes and ears as given for ass on page 87 and nostrils and teeth (pattern page 93). (7 pieces.)

1. Using grey felt prepare and cover two matchboxes (previously taped together) for body, a similar pair for front legs and neck combined, and a single one for hind legs working as given on page 17, no. 2 and Fig. 6 A, B and C, for Leviathan.

2. Noting position on picture, stitch body to neck/front legs.

3. Stitch edge of "hind legs" to lower back end of body so that it is loose and hinged—look at picture.

4. *Tail:* Roll felt round $\frac{1}{2}$ pipe cleaner and stab stitch all along one short end and the long edge as shown for serpent in "Joseph In The Pit", page 61, no. 18, and Fig 47, but have the felt $\frac{1}{2}$ inch (1·5 cm) longer than the pipe cleaner and fringe this piece. Sew to body.

5. *Head:* Make the head as given for Leviathan pages 16/17, nos. 4 and 5 and Fig. 6 E, F and G, using grey felt.

6. Stick eyes, ears and nostrils in place. Look at picture.

7. Stick teeth all round inside of upper jaw, thus propping it open a little.

8. Stick and stitch head to top of neck—note position; the ass has her head turned to look and laugh at Balaam. Stick on mane—to top of head, then twisting round to one side of neck because the head is turned. Tie on bridle and reins. Stick on saddle cloth.

FOR BALAAM YOU WILL NEED

A small empty cylinder (a plastic spice container was used for original), approximately 3 inches long × 1½ inches diameter (8 × 3·5 cm) for body.
Three lolly (popsicle) sticks for limbs.
Empty Smartie tube for head (or other small tube—it just needs to be less in diameter than the body tube).
Flesh felt for face, arms and legs.
Bright coloured felt for "tunic" and sleeves.
Scraps of black felt for eyes, red for nose, brown for sandals.
Brown wool for sandal straps.
Black wool for hair.
String for girdle.
A piece of twig for staff.

HOW TO MAKE HIM

1. Cut out sleeves, eyes and nose (patterns page 93). (5 pieces.)

2. *Head:* Cut 1 inch (2·5 cm) off the Smartie tube for head. Stuff with paper and cover with flesh felt—a strip round the edge and a circle at each end (Fig. 52 A and B).

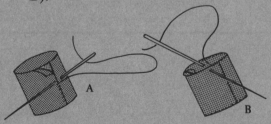

Fig. 52   Making Balaam's head.

3. *Body:* Cover the body cylinder in the same way, using bright felt but leaving one round end uncovered (seat end).

4. *Preparing limbs:* Cut the three lolly sticks in half with old scissors or a penknife and cover the six pieces by folding a piece of flesh felt round each one (Fig. 53 A) and stab stitching along the straight end, long side and curved edge (B), then trimming as necessary (C).

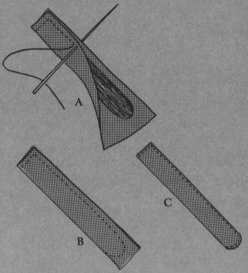

Fig. 53   Preparing lolly sticks for limbs.

5. *Legs:* Oversew two of the pieces together—a rounded end to a straight (Fig. 54 A). This is the knee—make sure that it is "hinged" and bends. Make another leg in the same way, then stick straight ends to base of cylinder (B) and stick a circle of felt to match tunic (the one you would normally have used whilst covering cylinder) over the top (C).

6. *Feet:* Break the two lower sticks 1 inch (2·5 cm) from rounded ends and bend forward for feet (look at picture).

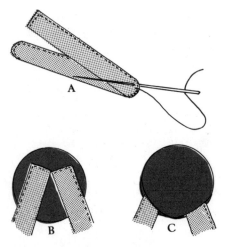

Fig. 54   Making legs.

13. Tie on a string girdle and sew a twig to right hand for a staff.

Fig. 55   Making Balaam's hair.

7. *Sandals:* Criss-cross wool from under feet up legs for sandal straps and stick a piece of brown felt under foot for soles, trimming to fit.

8. *Arms:* Break the other two covered sticks $\frac{3}{4}$ inch (2 cm) from the rounded ends for hands, and bend. Sew arms to body, noting positions—the right hand to hold a staff and the left twisting outwards to save himself from falling.

9. *Sleeves:* Stick sleeves over top of arms.

10. *Beard:* Sew on wool beard as given for Jonah, page 66, no. 4, Fig. 51 B.

11. *Hair:* Stick a bundle of wool from front to back of head for fringe and back hair (Fig. 55 A) and another from side to side to cover rest of head (B). Press firmly in place and trim.

12. *Face:* Stick on eyes and nose.

"And Balaam said unto the ass 'Because thou hast mocked me: I would there were a sword in mine hand for now would I kill thee.' And the ass said unto Balaam 'Am I not thine ass upon which thou hast ridden ever since I was thine unto this day? Was I ever wont to do so unto thee?' and he said 'Nay'."
(Numbers 22.29, 30)

A DANCING GIRL—
string puppet from spools

"The women came out singing and
dancing."   (1 Samuel 18.6)

There is no doubt that the women
of these times were a gay lot who
loved pretty clothes, jewelry, make-
up and dyed hair! We read of
Jezebel who painted her face, no
doubt using henna, and of the
vulgar extravagance of women
"with stretched forth necks and
wanton eyes walking and mincing
as they go".   (Isaiah 3.16)

At every excuse such as weddings,
harvests, victories, or the return of
travellers or warriors, there was
music and dancing. I thought a
good way of using up empty reels
and spools would be to turn them
into a simple dancing puppet. After
all there is " . . . a time to weep and
a time to laugh; a time to mourn
and a time to dance . . . a time to
read and a time to sew . . ."
          (Ecclesiastes 3.4, 7)

YOU WILL NEED

9 empty "Drima" reels (long slim
spools) for limbs and neck.
2 empty cotton reels for body.
A scrap of bright material for dress.
Piece of the top of old tights for
head and a handful of stuffing.
8 lolly (popsicle) sticks for hands,
feet and bars.
Black wool for hair.
Ribbon for head band.

Black, white and red felt for eyes,
nose and mouth.
Beads and brass curtain rings for
jewelry.
Sellotape (Scotch tape), glue and
strong black thread.

HOW TO MAKE HER

1. Cut out eye make-up, eyes,
pupils, nose and mouth (8 pieces),
patterns page 94.

2. *Head:* Make exactly as for
Joseph, page 59, no. 6, but push a
Drima reel into centre of gathers
instead of cane. Pull these up very
tightly and fasten off. (There is no
hole to stitch through as on cane.)
(Fig. 56 E).

3. *Hair:* Make as for Balaam,
page 72, no. 11, Fig. 55.

" . . . Well set hair . . ."
          (Isaiah 3.24)

4. *Face:* Stick on black eye make-
up, then white eyes, black pupils,
nose and mouth. Embroider
eyebrows, trying to give the eyes in
particular an artificial painted
appearance

" . . . though thou rentest thy face
with painting, in vain shalt thou
make thyself fair . . ."
          (Jeremiah 4.30)

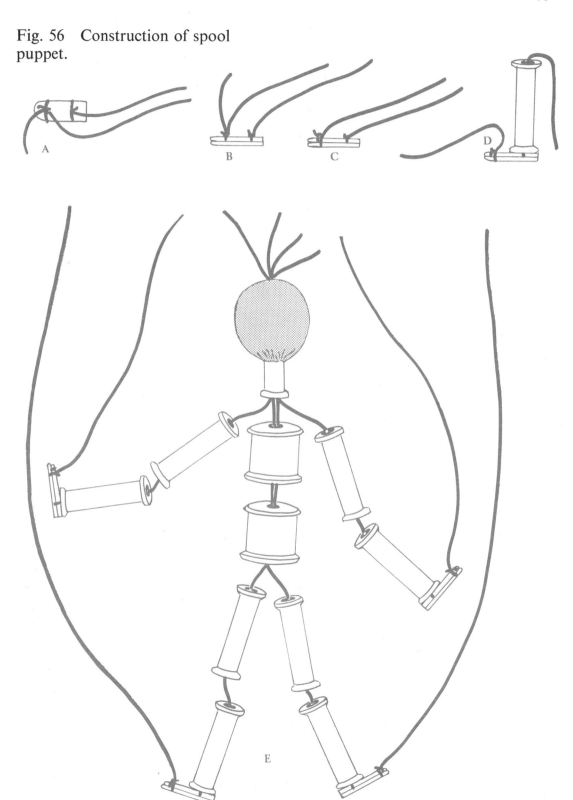

Fig. 56 Construction of spool puppet.

5. *Limbs:* Cut about 1 inch (2·5 cm) off each end of four lolly sticks so that you have eight short pieces each with a rounded end (hands and feet). Throw the middle sections away.

6. Take one of these and tie a piece of thread about one yard (91 cm) long round it at the straight end. Cut off short end of thread.

7. Take another similar piece of thread and tie round the same piece of lolly stick at the rounded end (Fig. 56 A).

8. Firmly glue another piece of lolly stick to the base of the piece with the threads attached (B).

9. Pass the string at the rounded end once round both the pieces of stick already glued together and tie securely on top. Cut off short end of thread. Dab the knots with a spot of glue or colourless nail varnish for security (C). Make three more pieces in the same way.

10. Thread each string nearest the straight ends into a long needle and pass this through a Drima reel. Glue the base of reel securely to top of each "hand and foot", having first removed the small round label from the end. Place on one side until absolutely dry and set (D).

11. Thread a second Drima reel on to each string (E).

12. *Body:* Pass the thread from two of the limbs (legs) together up through the holes in two cotton reels (E).

13. *Attaching arms and head:* Take the other two limbs (arms) and thread the strings from these and the two from the cotton reel body into one long needle. Pass this up through the hole in Drima reel "neck" and out on top of head (E). For clarity, the head is here shown without hair, etc.

14. Remove needle. Lay puppet on a table and carefully arrange limbs so that they will be loose enough to manipulate but are not too "gappy". Tie off threads very securely at top of head. Cut off two and leave two for attaching head to cross bar later. Secure knot with glue and tuck under hair.

15. *Dress:* With a piece of gay material make a "tube" about $4\frac{1}{2}$ inches long $\times 3\frac{1}{2}$ inches wide (11×8 cm). Slip on to puppet, and tucking raw edge inside, catch on each shoulder with a few strong stitches, arranging stitches between top of arms and neck. Pull in the waist a little with a loose gathering thread if you think it necessary— although in reality her tunic would probably have been long and straight, reaching well below the knee. (In our case this would hinder the puppet's movements.)

16. *Jewelry:* Hang a gilt chain or beads round her neck, stitching in place here and there so that they don't fall off. Add one or two small brass rings on wrists and ankles, taping them to the reels.
You can also add tiny earrings, and in real life she would probably have worn a jewel or ring in her nose and several in her hair, so add those if you wish.

" . . . The Lord will take away their tinkling ornaments about their feet . . . the chains and bracelets, the ornaments of the legs and the head bands . . . and the earrings . . . the rings and nose jewels . . ." (Isaiah 3.18–21)

17. *Stringing up:* Glue or bind four lolly sticks very securely together into a cross (Fig. 57 A).

18. Lay the puppet on a table and tie the string from top of head to centre of cross—make it as long as possible—according to whether you want your puppet to dance on the floor or a table. Tie the two strings from the feet, one to the back bar of cross and one to the front bar. These strings and the head string should all be level and taut when the "feet" are standing flat.

19. Tie the two arm strings one to each end of the side bars of cross, making them a little shorter than the leg strings.

Test your puppet. When you move the cross bars up and down from front to back she will kick her legs correspondingly in the most realistic way. Move them up and down from side to side and her hands will move gracefully—if the arm movement is not sufficient shorten these two strings a little. When you have your dancing girl as you want her, secure the strings to crossbar with Scotch tape or glue and tie a loop round centre cross so that you can hang her up when not in use and avoid muddling the strings.

Alternatively you can join your lolly sticks as Fig. 57 B. Attach head as before and leg strings to each end of long crossbar. Tie the hand strings together making one big "loop" from one hand to the other, hold this in one hand and manipulate it separately from the legs.

" . . . there is a feast in Shiloh . . . go and lie in wait in the vineyards . . . and see and behold, if the daughters of Shiloh come out to dance in dances, then come ye out of the vineyards and catch you every man his wife . . ." (Judges 21.19–21)

Fig. 57   Position of bars.

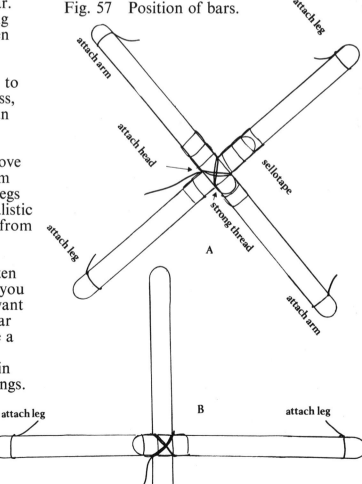

A KNITTED FISH

"Who shall give us flesh to eat?
We remember the fish which we
did eat in Egypt freely; . . ."
(Numbers 11.4, 5)

Many of the fish of the warm seas
of the Bible lands are fantastic
shapes and colours—fairy tale fish
indeed! Let's make a gay,
imaginative creature by simply
knitting three squares.

YOU WILL NEED

Oddments of wool (double knitting
is best) in as many different colours
as you like.
A pair of size 9 or 10 knitting
needles (USA 4 or 3).
Two white buttons and two black a
size smaller for eyes.
Cotton wool or kapok for stuffing.

HOW TO MAKE HIM

1. *Body:* Cast on 24 stitches.
Work in plain knitting and different
coloured stripes until you have a
perfect square. Cast off.

2. Make another square in the
same way.

3. *Tail:* Knit another smaller square
casting on only 12 stitches.

4. Fold this piece in half,
cornerways and oversew the two
open sides together, pushing just a
little stuffing in at the same time
(Fig. 58).

Fig. 58   Sewing up Fish's tail.

5. *Assembling:* Place the two large body squares together right sides inside, and oversew together all round except for about 1 inch (2.5 cm) each side of back "corner". Turn right side out.

6. On the right side stab stitch the two pieces together across the top and bottom "corners" (Fig. 59). These are the fins.

7. Stuff the rest of the body so that it is fat and moulded, leaving the fins flat.

8. Slip the point of tail into the opening at back end of fish and stab stitch right through body, tail and other side of body—thus closing opening and attaching tail (Fig. 60).

9. *Mouth and eyes:* Embroider the mouth with black wool and sew on buttons for eyes, the black on top of the white, and using white wool, work right through the fish from one side to the other so as to draw them in a little.

Amos thought up some pretty gruesome punishments for the Israelites—" . . . the days shall come upon you, that he will take you away with hooks and your posterity with fish hooks . . ." (Amos 4.2) So they were using hooks as well as nets in those far off Old Testament times!

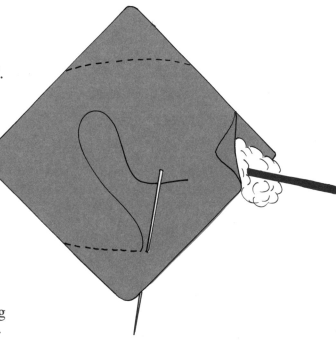

Fig. 59 Dividing off fins.

Fig. 60 Attaching tail.

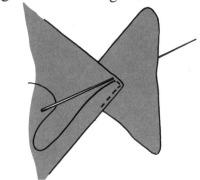

SAMSON AND DELILAH

" . . . Delilah said to Samson 'Tell me, I pray thee, wherein thy great strength lieth and wherewith thou mightest be bound to afflict thee . . . hitherto thou has mocked me and told me lies: tell me wherewith thou mightest be bound' and he said unto her 'If thou weavest the seven locks of my hair with the web.' And she fastened it with the pin." (Judges 16.6, 13)

Everyone knows the intriguing story of "strong man Samson" and his cunning lady friend Delilah. They are perfect subjects for model making.

FOR THE LOOM YOU WILL NEED

2 polystyrene "dishes" (sold containing chicken joints, mince, etc. in supermarkets). One about 5 inches (12 cm) square for base. One about 8 × 5 inches (21 × 12 cm) for the frame.
Some pins and bright coloured wool.

HOW TO MAKE IT

1. Using a sharp knife (or scissors) cut out the base of the rectangular dish, leaving a frame.

2. Cut a channel ¾ inch (2 cm) wide right across the base of the square dish, towards the back, leaving a wide "step" in front, on which Samson will sit.

3. Take some gay coloured wool and tie to one short edge of the frame; then wind the wool round and round from end to end about 12 times (making the warp ready for Delilah to weave her cloth), tie end to frame.—Cloth is called the "piece" or "web" when woven in this way.

4. On what will be the top of frame, secure each length of wool (with a pin pushed right up through each strand and the polystyrene frame, just so far that the point remains embedded and does not come out of the top edge. (A on picture).

5. Push the lower edge of frame into the slit on the square base and secure it there by pushing a pin through the frame, then the wool, then the base—working right along and pinning each strand of wool in turn. (B on picture).

In Old Testament times some of the looms used for weaving were upright rather like this one and some lay almost flat on the ground. Usually two women stood or crouched, one on each side, passing the shuttle backwards and forwards. Very different from our modern machines!

HOW TO MAKE SAMSON

1. Work as given for Balaam, page 70, but when cutting out omit sleeves and eyes so you will

A

B

need one pattern piece only—the nose. Work through nos. 2, 3, 4, 5 and 6 but cover half a lolly stick only for each arm.

2. *Arms:* Stick and sew an arm to each side, meeting in the centre front. Stick a piece of braid round base of tunic.

3. *Beard and hair:* Work as given for Balaam, page 72, nos. 10 and 11, but make the hair very long and thick. Arrange the long side pieces to cover ends of arms and stick in place.

4. *Face:* Stick on nose. Mark sleeping eyes with black ballpoint pen.

5. *Weaving:* Sit Samson on the "step" in front of loom, propped against one edge of frame—he is fast asleep. Take seven long strands of his hair and using a long needle weave each one across the warp. Knot them all together at the top and "fasten it with the pin"—a cocktail stick tucked through the knot and under the top of the warp.

" . . . Delilah said unto him 'The Philistines be upon thee, Samson.' And he awakened out of his sleep and went away with the pin of the beam and with the web . . ."
(Judges 16.14)

So once more he had mocked and deceived her.

FOR DELILAH YOU WILL NEED

2 cardboard tubes from toilet rolls. Bright felt to cover them } for her body.
Braid for decoration.
A Smartie or other small tube. } for head, hands and feet.
Flesh or fawn felt. }
Black wool for hair.
Narrow ribbon for headband.
1 brass curtain ring for bracelet.
1 gilt curtain hook for head ornament.
Scotch tape and tissue paper for stuffing.

HOW TO MAKE HER

1. Cut out hands, feet, eyes and pupils, collar (patterns page 88). (8 pieces).

2. *Body and head:* Join the two cardboard tubes together very firmly with plenty of Scotch tape. Cut a section off one end so that you have a tube about $6\frac{1}{2}$ inches (16 cm) long. Cut cardboard circles to fit ends and stuff the tube with crumpled paper. To avoid crushing, tape circles to ends. You now have a cylinder.

3. Cover this for body using bright coloured felt. Cut 1 inch (2·5 cm) off the Smartie tube for head and cover this with flesh-coloured felt as given for Balaam, page 71, no. 2, Fig. 52.

4. *Assembling:* Stick head to top of body and feet to base (look at picture).

5. Stick a piece of braid round top edge of each hand—slip a brass curtain ring on for a bracelet. Stick the completed piece to front of body. Look at picture. Her hands appear to be folded in front of her. Stick a piece of matching braid round base, i.e. hem of tunic.

6. *Hair:* Make this as given for Balaam, page 72, no. 11, Fig. 55. Stick a piece of narrow ribbon or braid round head for headband. Push a brass valance hook through front and stitch in place for her gold ornament.

7. *Face:* Stick on eyes. Mark black eyebrows, red nose and mouth using ballpoint pen.

8. *Collar:* Mark a pattern on the felt using bright coloured ballpoint or if you prefer, sew tiny beads on to form a pattern. Stick in place round front of neck.

" . . . Delilah said unto him, 'How canst thou say, I love thee, when thine heart is not with me? Thou hast mocked me these three times and hast not told me wherein thy great strength lieth.' "

(Judges 16.15)

MOSES in the bulrushes

" . . . his mother took for him an ark of bulrushes and daubed it with slime and with pitch and put the child therein and she laid it in the flags by the river's brink." (Exodus 2.3)

Note she hid it in the "flags"—not bulrushes! This is a simple little model that anyone can make easily.

YOU WILL NEED

2 polystyrene "dishes"—any size, (mine were 5×5 inches (12×12 cm)) for the river.
About 13 green cocktail sticks—or painted wood ones.
About 12 green pipe cleaners or white painted green for reeds.
$1\frac{1}{2}$ yellow pipe cleaners—or white painted yellow.
$1\frac{1}{2}$ brown pipe cleaners or white painted brown for bulrushes.
Bases of three small white plastic cream or yoghurt cartons for water lilies.
Scraps of yellow felt for "flags", green for lily leaves.
7 long pieces of garden bass or natural raffia.
A pair of *strong* unbreakable knitting needles size 9 (USA 4). } for basket.
A wooden ball, one pipe cleaner and white bandage for Moses.
Blue and green paint.

1. *The Basket:* if the bass is very thick split into two. *The Sides:* Cast on 16 stitches. K. 1 row: K.2

3. *Sewing up:* Push joins in bass through to the back. Join the two ends to one side A–B oversewing on wrong side and using cotton. Join on the second side all round A–B–B–A. Turn right side out.

4. *Moses:* Fig. 62. Double a pipe cleaner and push up into hole in ball, twist cleaner back on itself making the finished "baby" fit the basket A. Bandage all round him, fattening body as you work. Mark mouth and nose with red ballpoint, eyes and hair with black—after all he was 3 months old so probably had a little hair! (Exodus 2.2).

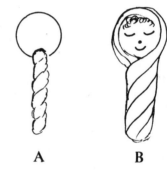

A   **B**

Fig. 62   Making Moses.

together at beginning of each row until 6 stitches remain: cast off: make another piece in the same way. These should be roughly the shape of Fig. 61 A.

2. *The Ends:* Cast on 5 stitches: K. 6 rows: K.2 together at beginning of next row: K. 1 row: K.2 together at end of next row: K. 3 rows: next row K.2 together K.1.: next row K.2: cast off. Knit another piece in the same way. These should be roughly the shape of Fig. 61 B.

Fig. 61   Shape of sides and ends of basket.

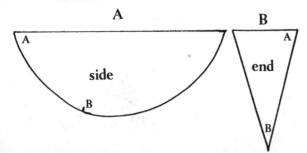

5. *The River:* Place one dish upside down and the other right way up on top of it. Paint the base of the top dish blue for water and all other pieces that show green for banks.

6. *Bulrushes:* Twist $\frac{1}{3}$ pipe cleaner round top of a green cocktail stick for each one. Paint brown. (See picture).

7. *Flags:* Cut out 2 or 3 shapes from yellow felt or paper (pattern page 87), stick to tops of green cocktail sticks. (Look at picture).

8. *Water lilies:* Fig. 63. Cut base from small plastic cream carton (A). Cut into flower shape (B). Bend petals upwards. Double half a yellow pipe cleaner, pierce hole in centre of flower, push cleaner through all but a little knob for centre of flowers, then push through one side of a circle of green felt for leaf (C). (It helps if you soak the plastic base in hot water beforehand).

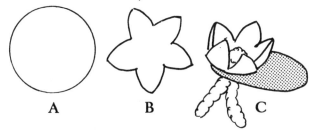

A   B   C

Fig. 63   Making a water lily.

9. *Assembling:* Lay basket containing baby in the river and add lilies, rushes, reeds and flags by sticking cocktail sticks into the polystyrene, some further than others to give different lengths. Pierce holes and push doubled green pipe cleaners into them—turning *doubled* side flat underneath. Pierce holes for lilies. Push yellow cleaners through and open and spread out at back. You have now secured the two dishes together without sticking! (Unless you use a special adhesive, sticking melts polystyrene.)

" . . . The daughter of Pharaoh came down to wash herself at the river . . . and when she saw the ark among the flags she sent her maid to fetch it . . ."   (Exodus 2.5)

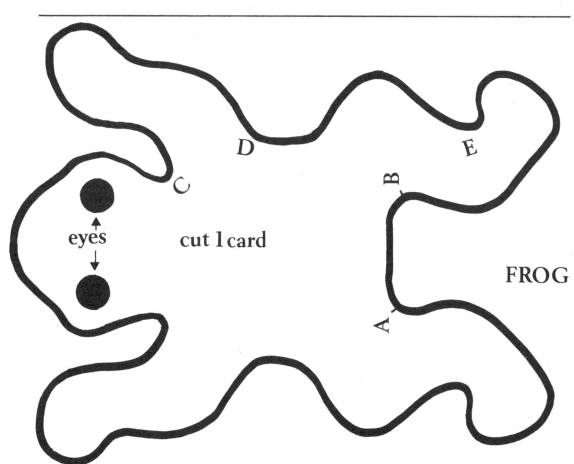

eyes

cut 1 card

FROG

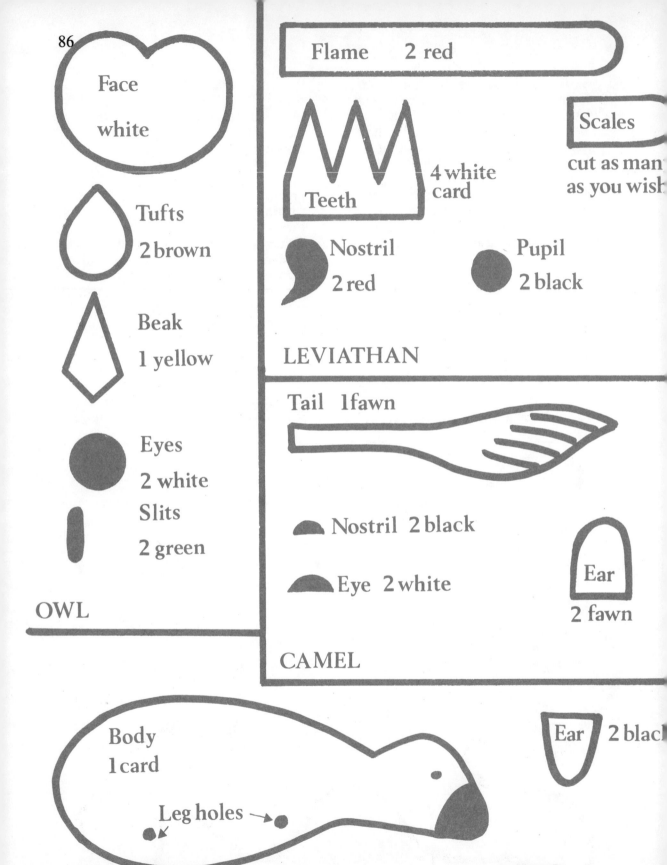

86

Face

white

Tufts

2 brown

Beak

1 yellow

Eyes

2 white

Slits

2 green

OWL

Flame   2 red

Scales

cut as man[y]
as you wish

Teeth   4 white
card

Nostril
2 red

Pupil
2 black

LEVIATHAN

Tail   1 fawn

Nostril 2 black

Eye 2 white

Ear
2 fawn

CAMEL

Body
1 card

Leg holes →

Ear   2 blac[k]

SHEEP

Tail 1 grey

Eye
2 black

Nostril
2 black

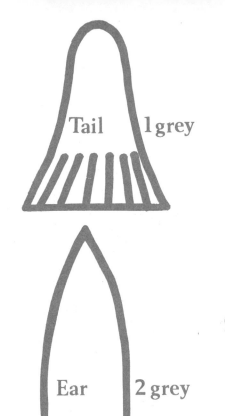

Ear 2 grey

Saddle bag strap
1 bright colour

ASS

Saddle
1 bright colour

Ear
2 brown

Iris (flags)

HORSE

MOSES

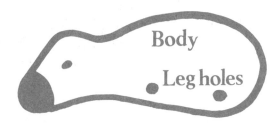

Body 1 card

Leg holes

LAMB

Ear
2 black

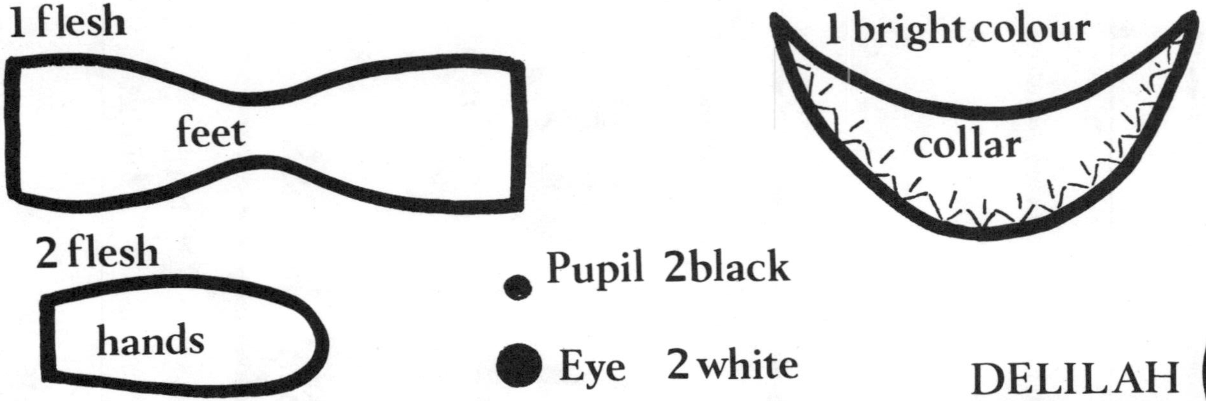

1 bright colour

collar

DELILAH

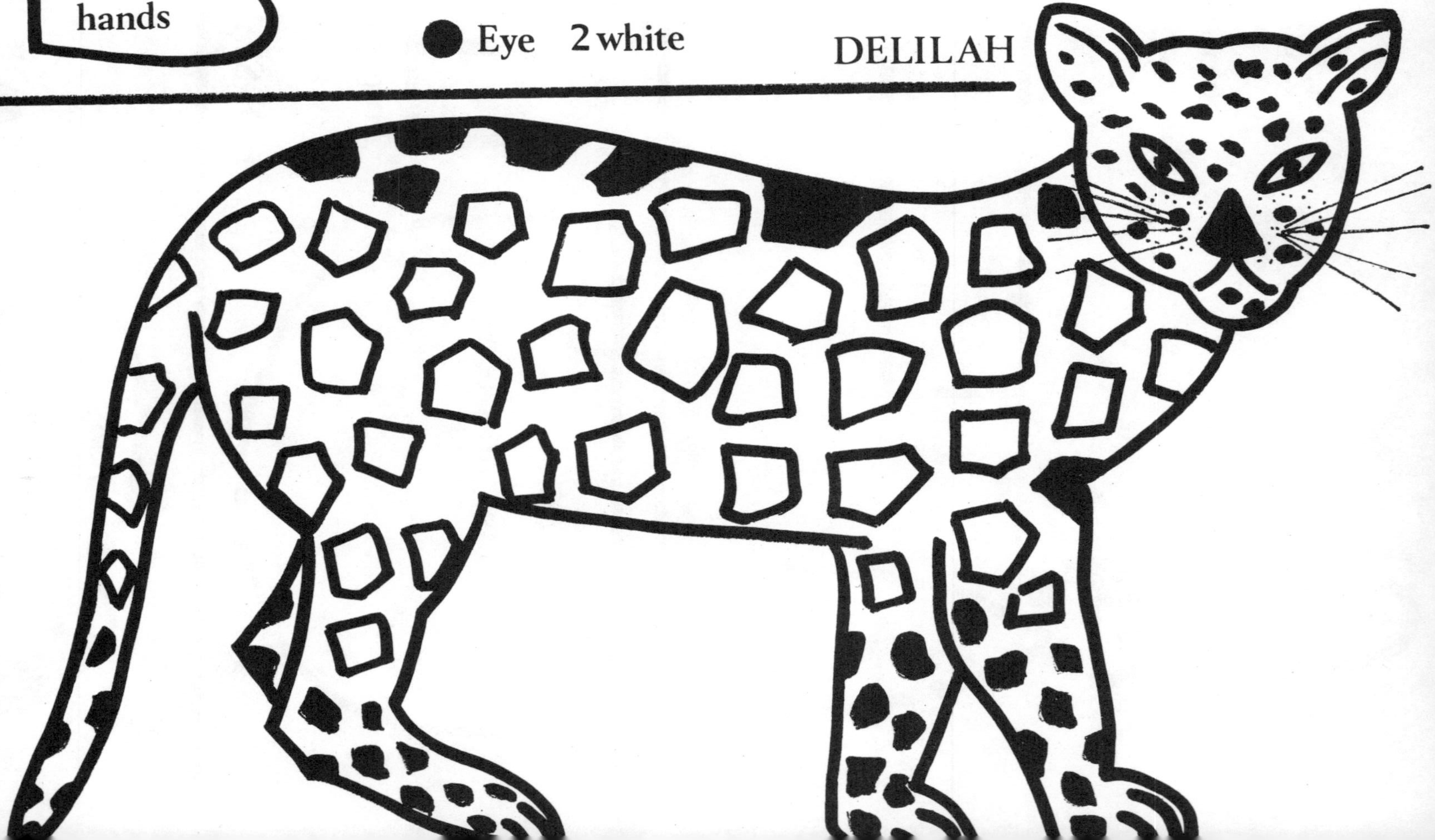

Pupil 2black

Eye 2 white

1 flesh

feet

2 flesh

hands

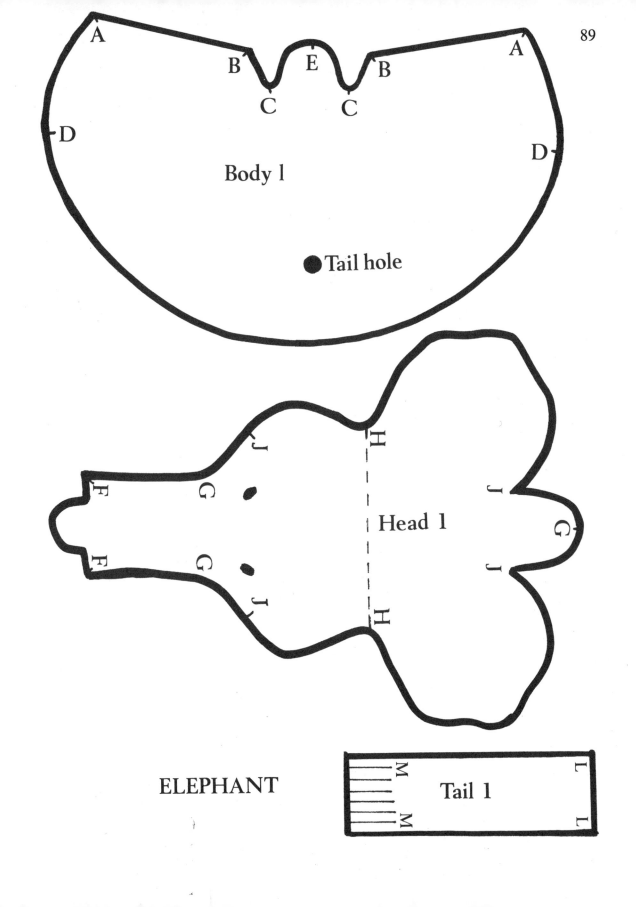

89

Body 1

●Tail hole

Head 1

ELEPHANT

Tail 1

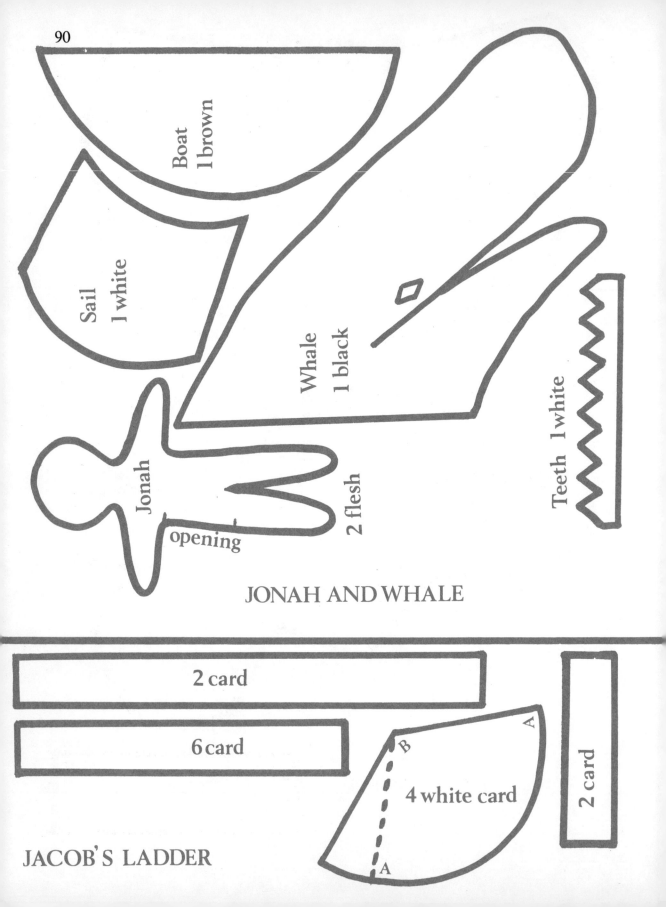

Boat
1 brown

Sail
1 white

Whale
1 black

Teeth 1 white

Jonah

opening

2 flesh

JONAH AND WHALE

2 card

6 card

4 white card

2 card

A

B

A

JACOB'S LADDER

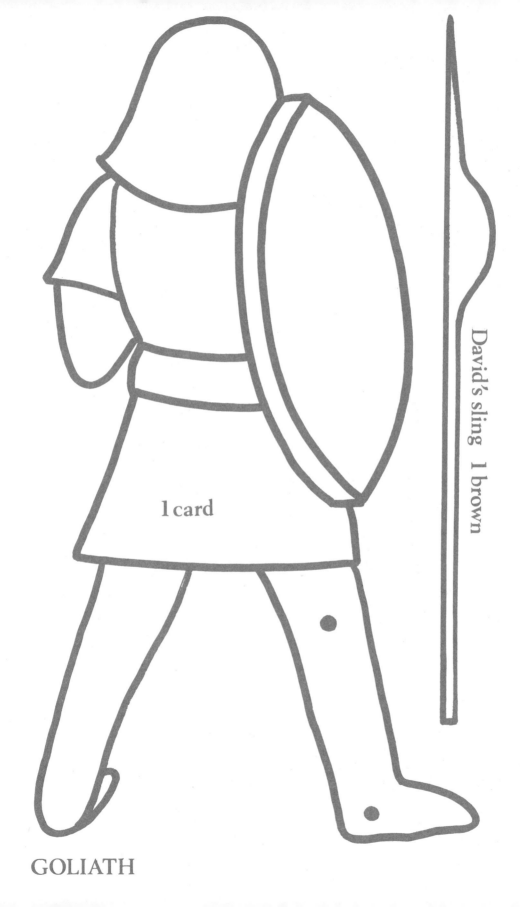

1 card

David's sling 1 brown

GOLIATH

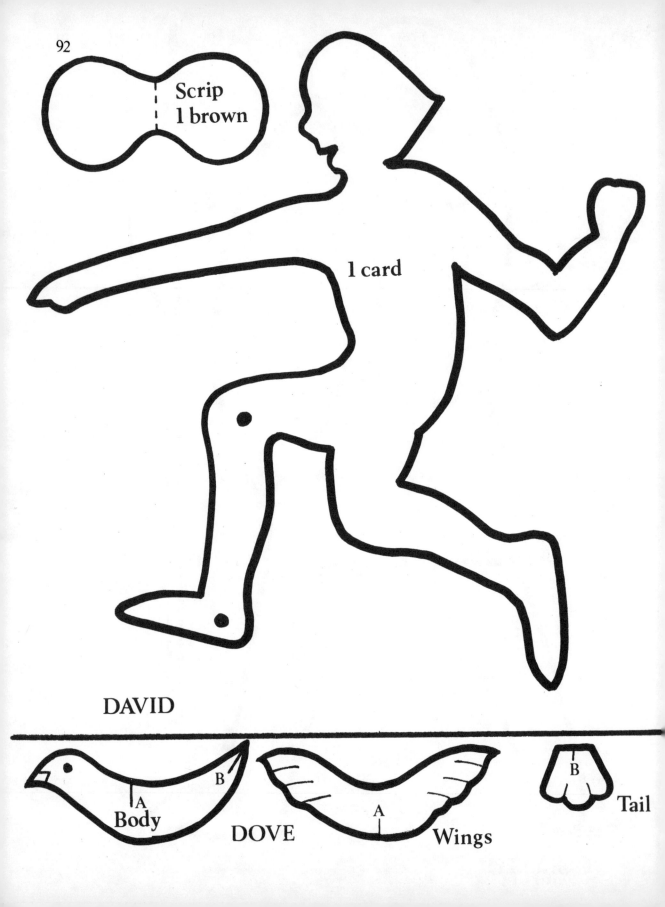

92

Scrip
1 brown

1 card

DAVID

Body
A
B

DOVE

Wings
A

B
Tail

Mouth 1 red

Hand

Nose
& Eye

1 red
2 black

2 fawn

JOSEPH

Wing

2 net

LOCUST

Sleeve

2 bright colour

● Eyes Balaam 2 black

● Nose 1 red

Ass's teeth   1 white

● Ass's nostril 2 black

BALAAM AND HIS ASS

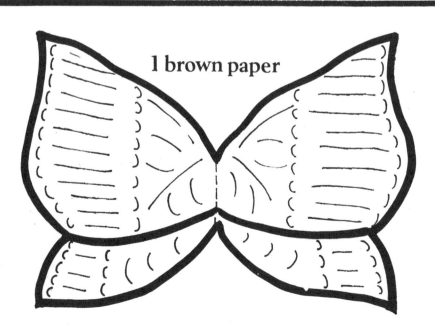

1 brown paper

MOTH

94

Tunic for Daniel and body of Lion

cut 2 for each

Eye make-up 2 black

Eye 2 white

Pupil 2 black

Nose 1 red

Mouth 1 red

DANCING GIRL

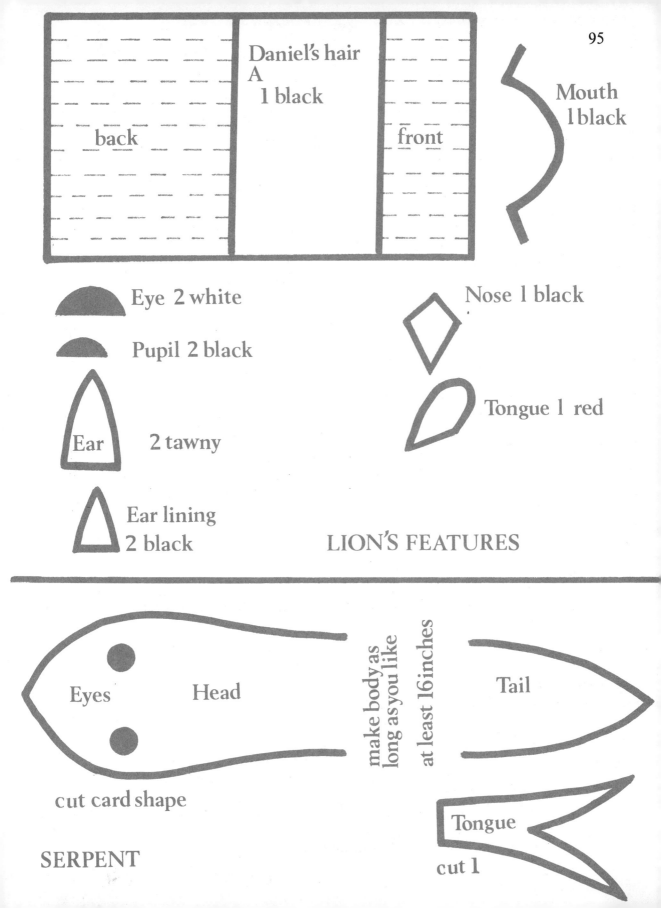

Daniel's hair
A
1 black

back

front

Mouth
1 black

Eye 2 white

Pupil 2 black

Ear   2 tawny

Nose 1 black

Tongue 1 red

Ear lining
2 black

LION'S FEATURES

Eyes   Head

make body as
long as you like
at least 16 inches

Tail

cut card shape

Tongue

cut 1

SERPENT

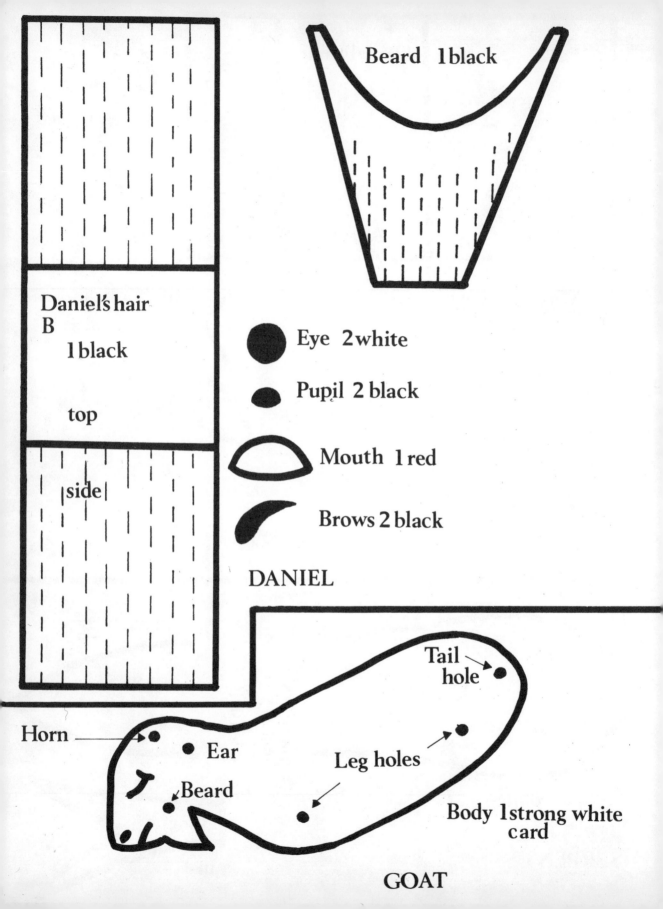

Beard 1black

Daniel's hair
B
 1 black

top

side

Eye 2 white

Pupil 2 black

Mouth 1 red

Brows 2 black

DANIEL

Tail hole

Horn

Ear

Beard

Leg holes

Body 1 strong white card

GOAT